# INTRODUCTION BY
# H.R.H. PRINCE CHARLES

**BUCKINGHAM PALACE**

I found it very encouraging having read some of the stories in this book, to see that a lot of the humour is directed at the Police themselves. I believe that this ability to laugh at oneself is an essential quality for survival in the over-stressed world of today. People who take themselves too seriously can turn what is an interesting experience into a very boring occasion. Tact and good humour correctly applied can, and often does, lighten a difficult situation and ease tension as many policemen will gladly testify.

Judging by some of the stories in this book I am convinced that policemen on the whole have the ability to see the funny side of themselves and I am sure that this is a great asset in the performance of their often difficult duties.

Some comedians (for example, Billy Connolly, Jasper Carrot, Max Boyce and Barry Humphries), do not in fact tell jokes but merely observe the funnier side of life and report it in a humorous style. Readers of this book will find many examples of the humour to be found in real life if one is prepared to look for it.

The proceeds of this book will go, not only to the Police Dependants' Trust, but also to the two Police Convalescent Homes. Many of you will be aware of the Police Dependants' Trust: a charity which has been in existence since 1966 when three policemen were murdered in Shepherds Bush. But I suspect that most of you have not heard of the two Police Convalescent Homes. The one at Hove is for the benefit of Police in Southern England, including the Metropolitan Police. The other, at Harrogate, caters for officers from the North of England and the Royal Ulster Constabulary who are either sick or suffering from injuries—and I remember being most impressed by the latter when I visited it a few years ago.

I am sure that all the readers of this book will join me in wishing members of the R.U.C. and the other Police forces in Britain a more peaceful future.

*Charles.*

# SPARE A COPPER

*'With malice towards none; with charity for all; with firmness in right, as God gives us to see the right.'*

*– Abraham Lincoln, March 4, 1865*

This collection of humour concerning police life and the 'law' in general has been compiled by Superintendent George Harris, MIPM, MInstPS, MBIM of the Derbyshire Constabulary.

**Police Dependants' Trust**
Patron: H.M. The Queen

All royalties from this book will be applied to the Police Dependants' Trust and other national police charities.

Previous publication by same author:

'A Policeman's Lot . . .'
Published 1979
by Police Review Publishing Co. Ltd.

ISBN 0 85164 000 1

©George Harris 1982

A Police Review Publication
Police Review Publishing Co.
14 St. Cross Street
London EC1N 8FE

# THE POLICE DEPENDANTS' TRUST

On August 12, 1966, at Shepherds Bush in London, Sergeant Head and Constables Fox and Wombell of the Metropolitan Police were murdered by armed criminals. Indignation at the crime and sympathy with the dependants of the victims found expression first in the immediate gift (anonymous at the time) by Sir William Butlin of £100,000 to set up a fund for helping the dependants of Police officers killed or injured on duty. This lead was quickly followed by a remarkable display of public generosity all over the country and contributions soon brought the fund over the £¼ million mark. A meeting of representatives of the Police Service was held on August 25, 1966, under the chairmanship of the late Lord Stonham, then Parliamentary Under Secretary of State and afterwards Minister of State at the Home Office, and it was accepted that the trust should be administered by representatives of the police for the police service.

The Police Dependants' Trust was constituted by the signing of the deed on December 21, 1966, and was registered with the Charity Commission in January, 1967. In August, 1967, the Trust was honoured by receiving the Patronage of H.M. The Queen.

A national appeal has been maintained with the object of securing a working capital of sufficient size to provide an income adequate to meet the requirements for the assistance of persons within the scope of the Trust. Although the response to the appeal has been good, the effects of inflation and the growing demands on the fund make it necessary constantly to build up the Trust's resources to ensure that they will be able to serve future needs.

# THE NORTHERN POLICE
# CONVALESCENT HOME, HARROGATE

The Northern Police Convalescent Home, St. Andrew's, is a registered charity supported by the voluntary subscriptions of members of the Northern Forces of England and Wales, Scotland and Northern Ireland.

St. Andrew's is a spacious friendly house standing in its own grounds in one of the most beautiful inland resorts in Europe. The house is fitted with comfortable furnishing and decorated in modern style. Everything is provided for the comfort, relaxation and care of the guests.

Although St. Andrew's is not a nursing home, all guests are under medical care. Medical officers and a consultant attend regularly and there is a fully qualified nursing sister on the Staff. Guests requiring physiotherapy or hydrotherapy are catered for at a private treatment centre and all types of diet are available.

The aim of St. Andrew's is to provide recuperative rest in an atmosphere of relaxation and enjoyment. It is not a condition to have been seriously ill or injured or to have had an operation to gain admittance.

As the Home is a registered charity its facilities and services are necessarily matters of bounty and not as of right and the committee have formulated certain regulations under the authority of the Charity Commissioners for the purpose of giving effect to the wishes of the founder (Miss Catherine Gurney) in the light of the changed conditions of modern times and to provide essential funds to meet the cost of so doing.

# THE CONVALESCENT POLICE
# SEASIDE HOME

The Police Seaside Home was established in 1890 by the late Miss Catherine Gurney, OBE (President of the International Christian Police Association), with the assistance of Miss Griffin, for the benefit of police officers of all ranks requiring rest and a change of air after sickness or injury.

In 1892-3 a new building was erected on freehold ground, the site being given by the late Miss E. M. Bell. The foundation stone of this building was laid in October 1892 by HRH Princess Christian, and the Home was opened in July 1893. After that date it was enlarged four times. On September 26, 1966, the Home moved to the new building at 205 Kingsway which was officially opened in November 1966 by H.M. Queen Elizabeth the Queen Mother.

The Home is now maintained by contributions from police officers serving in member forces, donations from both force and private sources and income from investments.

# FOREWORD

Humour is a funny thing, or, to avoid tortology, humour is a strange thing. The more serious a set of circumstances is, the more humorous anything funny emanating from it can be. This is borne out with some of the excellent humour which has come out of the services during wartime. It seems as though there is something within the human make-up which, in times of adversity, prepares the psyche to withstand extreme pressures by seeing the funny side of circumstances which certainly are not humorous. People steel themselves against adversity and turn to anything of humour. Even lower down the scale, in farce, many millions of people have laughed at the man slipping on the banana skin. What can be funny about someone slipping over and falling violently to the ground, with possible serious injury? Nothing, but that type of incident has evoked much laughter throughout the centuries.

I believe that it must be in this area that humour concerning the police and the law can, mainly, be classified. What is amusing about a man, hopelessly drunk being arrested by a policeman and appearing before the 'beak' the next morning? It's tragedy, but there must be many hundreds of jokes, anecdotes and funny stories built around a simple, but degrading, set of circumstances such as that.

Perhaps the subtle difference is between making fun out of the scenario and seeing the funny side of it, as I said earlier, to relieve the pressure of dealing constantly with the depressing acts of human beings. Often, too, a potentially dangerous situation can be diffused by a well-chosen, humorous remark. Humour is a great leveller!

A policeman's duty covers the whole span of human life. He can be there at the birth; all too often he is there at the death, sometimes very, very violent. Without being too cynical, I can say that when one traces the path from the cot to the grave there is a great deal of sadness and despair throughout the journey. When there is trouble, no matter of what kind, it is usually the policeman who, initially at least, has to deal with the situation. It is because of this that I would go so far as to say that, without a sense of humour, a policeman's lot would *not* be a happy one.

I am happy to report that it is my experience, over a period of 30 years, that there is a lot of humour in the British police officer, and long may it remain so.

I extend my heartfelt gratitude to all those who have helped and encouraged me in the compilation of this collection. Unfortunately space prevents me from mentioning everyone but some must be.

Firstly, my thanks to Doreen May, Brian Hilliard, Alina Grzenda and the staff of *Police Review*. Then to Pauline Vincent and Geoff Gregory, both civilian members of the Derbyshire Constabulary, for their clerical assistance.

My wife, son and daughter are also entitled to recognition for creating an atmosphere conducive to hours of laborious editing and two-finger typing.

*Supt G. A. Harris*

# LIST OF CONTENTS

# JOKES

I have said before that there are certain standard police jokes but there are often many variations on the same tale. For some years I thought that I knew pretty well all that had been 'cracked' about the police service, but still they continue to come in. I do not think that it is an accident that harder times give birth to more and often funnier material. I believe this to be true in respect of all humour but it is certainly so within the police service. Here follows a selection of these jokes.

### Les Dawson, TV and Radio personality

There's the one about the middle aged matronly lady who had a minor crash in her small saloon. The policeman, on the spot, said: 'What gear were you in madam?'

She replied: 'Surely you can see, can't you, twin set with woollen skirt and matching hat.'

*    *    *

A constable was also on the spot when a workman fell from the top of a 200 foot chimney. The bobby cradled the injured man's head and asked: 'What is your occupation?' The workman replied: 'Ex steeplejack.' The policeman asked: 'When did you quit that job?' The chap said bitterly: 'Halfway down!'

*    *    *

The local road safety officer gave a series of lectures on his subject to a club. He impressed on members that there was a need to be seen by other road users. He urged all present to wear something light and visible particularly during the dark winter evenings.

One member of the club was so impressed that one dreadful evening when he had to go out, he dressed himself completely in white—and was knocked down by a snow plough.

*    *    *

A police patrol was travelling northwards along the M6 in the centre lane when the driver saw, through the rear-view mirror, a six foot chicken with three legs catching up with the police car in the third lane. Eventually it passed travelling at 80mph. The police car gave chase and the chicken accelerated to 100mph. Gradually it increased its speed to 150mph with the police patrol having great difficulty in keeping up with it.

After some 30 miles the chicken slowed down considerably, crossed to the left of the motorway and departed by a slip-road; the car followed. The chicken continued along several miles of country roads until it turned into a farm yard. The police car drove in shortly afterwards with a screech of brakes. The chicken which had come to a halt was startled and took off again. A farmer came out and one of the officers said to him: 'I say, dad, you grow big chickens here and with three legs. What do they taste like?' 'Can't tell ye lad, they're too b..... quick for us to catch!'

*     *     *

**Steve Jones, TV and radio personality**
Early one morning a motor car which had certainly seen better days was being driven down the High Street when it was overtaken by a panda car and stopped. A constable climbed out of the police car and walked back to the driver's door of the other car.

The driver had wound down his window. 'Anything wrong officer?' he asked.

'Yes, sir. Your front nearside light is not working.'

'Oh I'll soon sort that out,' replied the driver. He got out of the car, went to the front and kicked the light-assembly—the light came on. 'All right then, officer, is that all?'

'Just one thing, sir, try giving the windscreen a kick and see if you can make a current excise licence appear!'

*     *     *

An American tourist struck up a conversation with a constable outside the gates of Buckingham Palace. The American was more than a little over-bearing and certainly boring, but the police officer remained cool and ultrapolite. 'You know, officer,' said the tourist, 'this here Palace of yours is certainly big but my ranch back in the States is large, real large. You listen to this. I can get up at dawn, get into my car and drive east and do you know by sundown I would still be on my land.' The constable thought for a second and then replied politely: 'Oh yes, sir, I remember once having a car like that myself!'

Unabashed the American continued: 'There's one thing I'll

give you officer, this here Palace has certainly got great lawns I'd sure like to know how they do it.' 'Quite simple', replied the constable, 'all they do is to dig the soil well. They turn it, level it and rake it several times. They buy the finest seed and spread it; then they roll it and leave it for some weeks. When the time is appropriate they mow the grass, they keep on mowing and mowing and then, in about four hundred years they have lawns just as you see them in the Palace ground!'

*          *          *

### Sir Kenneth Newman

The members of a police station situated in a fairly remote townland in Northern Ireland had gained a reputation for insobriety and inattention to duty. This came to the attention of Headquarters where it was decided that the inspector of the station should be changed. The newly appointed inspector was called to Headquarters and exhorted to improve the standard of discipline. The inspector took his instructions very seriously and arrived in the townland incognito, dressed in mufti. Seeing Constable Moriarty in the high street, he decided to test him. 'Tell me, constable,' he said 'is there a public house nearby?' 'Why, so there is sir' said Moriarty, 'and to be sure I will take you there myself.' Still setting the trap, the incognito inspector joined Moriarty in the bar and spent some time with him eating and drinking. Eventually, deciding to spring the trap, he said to Moriarty 'Tell me, what would your sergeant say if he walked in now.' 'Oh,' replied Moriarty, 'I suppose he would say "Now aren't you the fly one, Moriarty, a standing there eating and drinking with the new inspector".'

*          *          *

### R. T. M. Henry, MVO, OBE, QPM, CPM, Royal Hong Kong Police

#### Get priorities right

There was the sad occasion when by coincidence the Pope and a chief constable both died on the same day.

They both arrived at the Pearly Gates and St. Peter looked out and on seeing the chief constable immediately invited him to enter and asked the Pope to hang on for a minute. St. Peter immediately rolled out a red carpet, summonsed a Rolls Royce and ushered the chief constable into it for immediate despatch into heaven. He then turned back to deal with the Pope who was somewhat taken aback and indeed rebuked St. Peter for offering such VIP treatment to a chief constable ahead of himself, the Pope.

St. Peter was overcome with embarrassment and drawing the Pope quietly to one side said: 'Well you see, Holy Father, it is like this. Up here we have got lots of Popes, but this is the first time we have seen a chief constable.'

*     *     *

### Alan Towers, BBC Television

Patrolling the High Street one night a constable shone his torch into a shop doorway and found a couple kissing in the corner. In an attempt at humour he said: 'Hurry up, it's my turn next.'

With that the young man broke away and began to run.

The constable shouted: 'What's the matter lad?'

'I'm off,' he shouted, 'I've never been kissed by a copper before and I'm not going to start now!'

*     *     *

'He was as drunk as a judge.'

Judge: 'Don't you mean as drunk as a Lord?'

'Yes my Lord.'

*     *     *

Derby County were playing Manchester United at the Baseball Ground. The match was in progress but there was more action on the terraces. The home supporters were trying to get at the visitors but were kept apart by a line of police. Bottles were being thrown in both directions. One diminutive man was obviously concerned for his safety and he shouted to a nearby constable: 'What about all these bottles, someone's going to get hurt.'

The constable turned to him and said philosophically: 'Look mate, if one's got your name on it, that's it.'

Ducking and weaving the man replied: 'That's what worries me, my name's Worthington.'

*     *     *

Lord Birkenhead had a particular dislike of being told by judges that they had a poor opinion of his case. One such judge said to him: 'I have read your case, Mr Smith, and I am no wiser now than I was when I started.' To which Mr Smith (Lord Birkenhead) retorted: 'Possibly not, my Lord, but far better informed.'

Lord Darling dealt with a certain witness who said that he had been wedded to the truth since infancy by asking him how long he had been a widower.

*         *         *

## Who are the Jones's?

John Black and Alex Summers had been friends, colleagues and rivals for many years, in fact since the day they both joined the police service. They had struck up a friendship in the recruiting office of that southern force. Eventually their paths had separated when, upon promotion, they had transferred to different forces.

From time to time their paths crossed; they met at conferences, went to national sporting events and even attended the same courses at the Police Staff College. Both did particularly well and it was only a matter of time before they each became chief constable of a county force. By coincidence they were appointed on the same day in neighbouring counties.

Naturally, as time went by their friendship strengthened as they met more often. They met in their own homes and their wives were friendly disposed to one another. One afternoon Black's wife, June was entertaining Alex's wife, Ruth, to tea when the question of relative status came up.

June said that she could not understand why the Police Authority in their county provided her husband with a Jaguar car while the Police Authority in Ruth's county only provided her husband with a Ford. Ruth was taken aback more than a little.

So much so that that evening she made such a point of it to her husband he promised to attempt to persuade his Authority to provide him with a more prestigious vehicle. It took many months and many committee meetings but eventually Alex was delivered of a shiny new Jaguar.

At their next get-together Ruth could hardly wait to announce the news to June. Her triumph was short-lived; as soon as she had imparted her news she had to listen to June's news; John had been supplied with a brand new BMW which was certainly 'up-market'. The battle had now been commenced.

Alex was happy with his Jaguar but Ruth certainly was not! He must have a better car at all costs.

Alex wanted a peaceful life so he set about convincing his

Authority that the Jaguar he had so recently acquired was not quite right for the job and did not really befit his position in the community. He knew it would be a long, uphill struggle. It certainly was. The meetings went by without success and all the time Ruth's desire to keep up with the Blacks intensified.

All seemed hopeless and then there came a change in the political composition of the Authority and at the next meeting permission was granted for the chief constable to have a Mercedes.

Ruth could not wait for her next tea party with June to pass on the information. She was disappointed when she found that both John and June were out so she left a message for June to ring her as soon as possible. Within a few minutes the telephone rang; it was June. June explained that her daughter had taken Ruth's message and passed it on. She went on to explain that she was ringing on the telephone which John's Police Authority had recently had installed in his official BMW.

This was too much for Ruth; her breath taken away she just rang off without passing on her snippet of information.

As can be expected there was but one topic of conversation in the Summers household that evening. Alex had been tolerant but now was the time for a few home truths. No way was he going to his Authority to have a telephone installed in his official car; no way.

There was only one way, thought Ruth, she would have to pay for a telephone to be installed in her husband's car herself. It was a few weeks before Christmas and this would be his Christmas present. On December 24 it was installed. That night she insisted that they went for a drive and no sooner was she on the road she demanded that her husband dial John's number. An unfamiliar voice answered. 'I would like to speak to your chief constable,' requested Alex. 'Sorry sir,' came the reply, 'he's engaged on the other line!'

Ruth's Christmas was in shreds but she was determined to have another go. On Christmas morning she insisted, once again, on going for a drive. Within minutes Alex was dialling John's car. An answer came quickly; it was the same voice as the previous evening. 'I suppose your chief is on the other line,' he said. 'No,' came the reply, 'he's having a shower.'

★    ★    ★

A chief constable was seconded to one of the Gulf States for six months to re-organise its police organisation. Eventually he returned after his secondment. He landed at Heathrow and was met by his driver at the terminal.

As was his style he sat in the front of the car with his driver.

'Everything OK, George?' he asked.

'Perfect,' replied George. 'Perfect . . . oh, there's just one thing, we had to bury your dog.'

'What do you mean, the dog was in perfect health when I left.'

'Yes, sir, we had to bury the dog after your horse kicked it to death.'

'But my horse was placid, why did it kick the dog?'

'It must have been the rafter that fell from the roof.'

'Yes, but why did the rafter fall?'

'Well you see, sir, the stable roof was on fire.'

'How then did the stable come to be on fire?'

'We think, sir, that it must have been a spark from your house when it was burning down!'

'Oh no!, what happened to the house?'

'We are not sure, sir, but we think that it was caused by the candle falling off your wife's coffin. Anyway you shouldn't be too bothered there's some good news: the heat was so intense that the daffodils came up two weeks early!'

*       *       *

There had been a series of inner-city disturbances and it had taken a toll on the hard worked constables who were in the front line. The next night it was just the same. The shields were out, the rioters were getting more and more in a violent mood. Suddenly one of the constables 'lost his bottle', he'd had enough; he ran. In fact he ran for about half a mile. He was stopped by another policeman.

'Look lad, I know it's bad, it's awful, but you've got to get back in there and help your mates.'

'No way; I've had enough, I'm not going back—no way.'

'Now see here, no man of mine is going to opt out like this, get back.'

'Look sergeant, I've had it . . .'

'Just a moment lad, I'm not your sergeant—I'm your superintendent!'

In one county force an assistant chief constable retired and the vacancy was advertised. Eventually his successor was appointed by the Police Committee. Shortly before he was due to commence duty the chief constable suggested to his deputy that it might be nice to welcome the new assistant by arranging a social get-together. They hit upon the idea of arranging a day's fishing by boat on a nearby river. The day came and all three set out for the centre of the river with their fishing tackle.

It was a hot morning and as the day progressed it became hotter and hotter. Soon after noon the deputy suggested that an ice-cold drink would be acceptable and they all agreed. The deputy stood up in the rowing boat, stepped over the side, walked across the top of the water and up to the grass bank to a nearby cafe. He soon returned with a tray of drinks, down the bank, across the top of the river and into the boat. The new assistant looked on amazed and thought to himself that such a thing had not happened for nearly two thousand years. He sipped his drink and kept quiet.

About an hour had passed and the chief constable decided that another drink was necessary. He stood up, stepped over the side of the boat, walked across the water up the bank and disappeared into the cafe. He emerged shortly with a tray of drinks and retraced his steps to the boat, once again walking over the top of the water. The assistant chief constable gratefully accepted the drink with hands which were shaking more than a little. Twice in an hour.

After another hour he plucked up his courage and said that it was his turn to buy the drinks. He stood up in the boat, stepped over the side and promptly sank.

The deputy turned to the chief constable and said: 'Shouldn't we have told him about the stepping stones?'

The chief constable replied: 'Which stepping-stones?'

\*        \*        \*

A constable was driving along a lonely country road early one winter's morning when he saw in front of him a blackbird lying in the road. It was a very cold morning, there was snow, frost and ice everywhere and it was obvious that the bird was suffering from the cold and was surely dying. Just at that moment a local farmer drove a herd of cows down the lane. One of the cows dropped a 'patty' and went on its way. The constable saw that this was a source of heat so he carefully picked up the bird and placed it on the pile. He then went on his way.

Only a few seconds passed and the heat had its effect. The bird moved, then got to its feet, started to sing and then strut around. A fox leapt from the hedgerow, caught the bird and ate it.

This story has three morals. Firstly, it is not only your enemies who drop you into it and secondly it is not only your friends who get you out of it, but, most importantly of all if someone does get you out of it never make a song and dance about it!

\*          \*          \*

It would be a mistake to think that all humour connected with the service is pro-police. Fortunately the examples are fairly rare; just three quick one-liners:

Notice: 'Help the police—beat yourself up.'

Critic: 'We have the best police force money can buy.'

Snide comment: 'A successful police force is one which catches more criminals than it employs.'

\*          \*          \*

The chief constable was invited to speak to the local chamber of commerce. It was a good speech and very well received. After the event the chief constable sought out the local reporter and asked him not to report the several humorous anecdotes he had used because he wished to use them at other functions.

The chief awaited the report in the next edition of the paper. He was more than a little disturbed when he opened the paper and read: 'The chief constable was the main speaker at a recent meeting of the chamber of commerce. As usual he made an excellent speech but some of the tales he told cannot be repeated here!'

\*          \*          \*

## Alf Parrish, Chief Constable of Derbyshire

A young, attractive mother was concerned about the manner in which 'bus drivers were driving rather recklessly across the pavement outside her house. She was so incensed that she wrote to the local divisional headquarters complaining.

A few days later an inspector arrived to follow-up the complaint. She invited him into the house, and went on to explain that the best view of the subject of the complaint could be obtained from her bedroom. Accordingly she took the inspector to the room and sat him on the bed. A little while passed and the young mother said that she must leave to fetch her eldest from school. The inspector said that he would remain in the room in the hope of getting a result.

He had been there for about 15 minutes when the woman's husband returned and came into the bedroom.

'What the hell do you think you're doing?' he asked.

'Oh, I'm waiting for a 'bus,' replied the inspector.

*          *          *

When I was preparing my previous book *A Policeman's Lot* . . . the profits from which were to be given to the Police Dependants' Trust, I was interviewed many times on television and radio.

At one interview which was for radio and was being recorded down the line (me in one studio and the interviewer in another), the interviewer could not have heard me properly because he asked me just what was a police defendant's truss!

*          *          *

He was the sort of constable who, if he saw any trouble, preferred absence of body to presence of mind!

*          *          *

**Bob Monkhouse, television and radio comedian**
There was the successful Fraud Squad Officer who got his twisters in a nick!

*          *          *

A young policeman, very keen, acquired a few books on the law such as Archbold's 'Criminal Pleading' and Stone's Justices' Manual. However after numerous attendances at various courts and listening to the pleas and arguments put forward by legal gentlemen, he realised that his little collection of books was deficient in that he had no copy of Grimm's Fairy Tales!

*          *          *

Once upon a time there was a particularly keen solicitor—he named his daughter Sue!

*          *          *

A court case in Alaska. Prosecuting Counsel to witness: 'Where were you on the night of October 26th to March 4th?'

The drunk had been thrown out of the public house several times but each time he staggered back into the bar. The local policeman explained to him thus: 'You must be putting far too much back spin on him!'

\*       \*       \*

Police Officer: 'I'm sorry, sir, but we have information which leads me to believe that you have pornographic literature in the boot of your car.'

Driver: 'It's a lie, I haven't even got a pornograph.'

\*       \*       \*

### David Kossoff

A very ancient piece of Jewish humour:

The elderly Rabbi of a small town in Russia long ago was constantly bedevilled by his flock coming to him with their troubles. They disturbed his meals, his rest and his sleep, for he cared. Everyone had trouble—a peck'l of woe. 'Nobody', they would tell him, 'has a worse peck'l than me.' One day he called the townspeople together. 'On Sabbath Eve,' he told them, 'you can all bring your peck'ls to the door of my house and leave them. For the whole of the Sabbath you can be free. The day after come back and you can take away any peck'l you like. On the morning of the day after the Sabbath the wise old Rabbi got up early. The townspeople came and stood and looked and considered. Then each took away his own peck'l. The Rabbi smiled and went back to bed.

(This philosophy might commend itself to some community police officers!)

\*       \*       \*

### Her Honour Judge Jean Graham Hall

A quotation from Adlai Stephenson, which I sometimes reflect upon in court listening to counsel: 'He suffers from nothing that lockjaw would not cure.'

\*       \*       \*

An Irish police officer approached his Building Society to obtain a mortgage for prospective house purchase. Upon being asked whether the property was semi-detached the officer replied: 'No—it's one of a block of two!'

An insurance agent confidence trickster was asked by the detective inspector how he could have cheated so many people who had placed their trust in him.

He replied: 'I couldn't if they hadn't!'

\*       \*       \*

**Max Bygraves, Comedian**
'Breathe into this bag,' said the copper.

The fellow blows into the bag and a big horn appears on his forehead.

The cop in disbelief says: 'Do that again!' The fellow blows again and a second horn appears.

The copper said: 'What have you been drinking?'

'Bovril,' replied the driver.

\*       \*       \*

A surgeon, a lawyer and a politician were dining in their London club. Over port one put the following question: 'I wonder which of ours is the oldest profession.'

The surgeon claimed his must be the oldest because in the Book of Genesis it is explained that God made Eve from one of Adam's ribs, which must have required a surgical operation.

After a pause the lawyer staked his claim. He said that God made order out of chaos which must have required the assistance of a legal mind.

But the politician won the day for was it not one of his breed that had created the chaos?

\*       \*       \*

Four superintendents' wives were having coffee together when they started to discuss their various vices.

The first explained that each day after her husband had left for the office she would take out a bottle of sherry and spend a good part of the day drinking.

The second admitted that her husband was a staunch no-smoker, so while he was away she would chain-smoke.

The third blushed rather when she explained that she wasn't averse to inviting tradesmen into the house.

At that the fourth wife got up from the table and prepared to leave. The other three demanded to know her vice.

She explained: 'I'm an uncontrollable gossip!'

**Terry Wogan**
What's black and blue and floats upside down on the Liffey?
    An Englishman caught telling 'Irish' jokes . . .

                    *        *        *

**Eddie Braben, scriptwriter**
A young lady, very distressed, staggered into the police station
and spoke in a trembling voice to the station sergeant: 'I've just
been attacked by a man in the park.'
    Sergeant: 'Can you give me a description?'
    Girl: 'It's about two miles long, half a mile wide with a
bandstand in the middle.'
    Sergeant: 'Right, we'll have the park arrested and brought in
for questioning!'

                    *        *        *

A beggar knocked at the door of a house and said to the woman
who came to the door: 'Lady, I'm down on my luck, I haven't
eaten today, I didn't eat yesterday and I didn't eat the day
before that . . .' He then saw a policeman's helmet hanging in the
hall. He continued '. . . and I don't care if I never eat again!'

                    *        *        *

**John Cleese, television personality**
The only legal story that comes to mind amused me a great deal
when I first heard it as a law student because it seemed to me to
indicate very clearly what tenuous connections some aspects of
the law have with the real world. It concerned a professor of law
at Cambridge who was a member of Trinity College.
    The College had got itself in a great difficulty having elected a
new Master. The Master announced that he would only take up
his position if he could bring his two dogs with him. This posed
a serious and heart-rending crisis at the College as the statutes
governing the College, from the 16th century of course,
specifically and categorically banned the entry of dogs into the
College. An emergency meeting of the College staff was held to
find a way through this impasse. They debated for two hours in
vain and then the Professor of Law arrived and asked what was
wrong. They explained the hopeless situation to him. 'Oh,' he
said, 'that is an easy one. Let us now pass a supplementary
statute deeming the Master's two dogs to be, for the purpose of
the Elizabethan statute, legally cats.' And so they did and the
problem ceased to exist.

The smoking room of the chief constables' club in London was fairly deserted at that hour of the morning. Two chief constables were sitting together making conversation, while, at the opposite end of the room was a lonely figure sitting in an armchair reading a newspaper. One of the chief constables said: 'You know, I think that is the Archbishop of Canterbury over there.'

'Never' replied his colleague.

'I'm sure it is. I am so sure that I'm willing to bet you £50.'

'You're on' was the reply.

The bet having been agreed, it was decided, after some argument, that the only way to settle the issue was to seek confirmation from the person concerned, and that it should be decided by the spin of a coin. The chief constable who had made the initial 'identification' lost the toss and accordingly approached the mystery man with a politely worded enquiry as to whether or not he was the Archbishop of Canterbury.

'Mind your own B....y business,' was the testy reply.

The enquirer returned to his colleague. 'The bet's off, we'll have to call it a draw,' he said, 'the blighter wouldn't tell me!'

*        *        *

Sometimes it is doubted whether there remains any witchcraft in Scotland. Perhaps this removes the doubt.

A constable was driving a panda car in a very remote part of the Highlands when he saw a particularly attractive young woman thumbing a lift at the side of the road. He stopped and picked her up. It turned out that she was a witch. They travelled along the road for half a mile when she touched his knee and he turned into a lay-by!

*        *        *

A jeweller's shop in Dublin was robbed in broad daylight and Pat, an eye-witness, rushed to the police station. 'I saw it all,' he said, 'and, man, ye'll never believe it! There was this damned great elephant comes lumbering down Grafton Street, smashes the window with his tusks, puts in his trunk, scoops out all the jewellery and away he goes.'

'I've never heard the like of that before, was he an Indian elephant or an African elephant?'

'How do ye tell the difference?' asked Pat.

'Well, you see,' said the sergeant, 'an Indian elephant has wee small ears which he keeps close to his head, but an African elephant has great big floppy ears which stick out. Which sort of ears did this fella have?' 'Oh, I couldn't tell ya that,' said Pat, 'sure, wasn't he wearing a stocking mask.'

★          ★          ★

A policeman had been playing for the force team and had dislocated his shoulder. He was taken to the local hospital and placed on a bed in the casualty ward. A few minutes later a sister came in with two porters. While the porters held the policeman down the sister with a swift snatch put the shoulder back into place. The constable let out a tremendous cry of pain. The sister looked at him and said:

'A big man like you and you can't stand pain. Let me tell you that a few minutes ago I was with a woman when she gave birth without even a murmur.'

'Just you try and put it back into place,' he replied, 'and see what sort of reaction you get from her!'

★          ★          ★

A security guard stopped a West Indian worker as he left a cigarette lighter factory. He said to him: 'We are having a spot check, have you any lighter parts?'

'No man, I'm this colour all over,' replied the West Indian.

★          ★          ★

A constable attempted to stop a car one evening but it drove by him and sped off. A chase ensued and eventually the driver was stopped. The constable examined the car and found it to be in an advanced state of dilapidation. Everything was wrong from completely bald tyres to dangerous bodywork; in all the constable listed 20 offences in respect of which he intended to report the driver.

As he was taken away the driver remarked: 'It wasn't really worth nicking, was it?'

★          ★          ★

A horse-box exceeding the limit on the M4 was stopped by a motor patrol. The driver of the horse-box excused himself saying that he was on his way to the races and was very, very late. The constable being of a sporting nature asked if he could see the horse. The driver climbed out of his cab and went to the rear. He opened the door to reveal an empty box. The constable asked for an explanation to which the driver replied: 'Well someone has to carry the non-runners!'

*       *       *

**The late Ted Ray**
Police Constable Johnny Davis was allowed to go off duty an hour early. He dashed off home and, as he had already had his supper, he went straight upstairs and into his bedroom. He heard steady breathing and so that he would not waken his wife Caroline he undressed in the dark. She sighed and snuggled her body to his. He joyfully responded and then she whispered 'Johnny'. 'Yes dear,' he replied.

'I have a dreadful headache,' she murmured, 'be a darling and pop down to the all-night chemist and get me some asprin. Don't switch the light on, my head is throbbing.'

He got out of bed dressed in the dark and went downstairs and out to the chemist's shop.

The chemist handed over the aspirin and said: 'You feeling all right?'

'Of course,' answered Johnny, 'why not?'

'It looks as though *you* need the aspirin,' remarked the chemist, 'otherwise why the hell are you wearing a fireman's uniform!'

*       *       *

The police are looking for a man with one eye called **Murphy**.
   'What's the other eye called?'

*       *       *

   The police are looking for a man with one eye—typical inefficiency!

*       *       *

The police want a tall, handsome man for **assault on an** attractive young woman.
   'What's the salary?'

*       *       *

A woman driver drove through the town in such a manner that other drivers drove on to the pavement and pedestrians ran into doorways. She went the whole length of the High Street swerving from side to side, the car eventually coming to rest a few inches from the rear of a stationary bus. A policeman had seen this happen and with a measured tread he approached the driver.

In an ultra-polite manner he said: 'I hope you won't mind waiting a few minutes while I walk back up the High Street. I would like to place my handkerchief in the centre of the road. When I have done that I shall return here and ask you kindly to drive back up the street in the same manner as you came down but this time, please see if you can pick up my handkerchief in your teeth.'

★     ★     ★

A police patrol was travelling along the M4 when they were passed by a Mercedes travelling in excess of 100mph. The police car slipped into the fast lane and started to catch up with the offending car. A doctor was driving the Mercedes and when he saw through the rear-view mirror who was following him he slowed down to 70mph. As the police car pulled level he dangled his stethoscope for the constables to see. Thinking that the doctor was on his way to an emergency they pulled back and allowed him to continue unhindered.

A couple of hours later the same police car was on the opposite carriageway when once again they were passed by the doctor in his Mercedes once more exceeding the 'ton'. The doctor quickly realised his mistake and again, as the police car drew level, he raised his stethoscope. This time, however, the observer in the police car raised a pair of handcuffs and indicated that the doctor should pull on to the hard-shoulder.

★     ★     ★

An Arab sheik had amassed a fortune through oil. He had many daughters but only one son, a 14-year-old, the apple of his eye.

He decided that he wanted to give his son everything he wanted, but his son wasn't particularly interested. One day his father called him to his presence and asked him what he could buy for him.

The son replied that he would like his own house. The sheik replied that that would be easy, he would buy his son a mansion in America, a chateau in France and a castle in England, but surely there was something else he would like. The son replied that he wouldn't mind owning a car so his father arranged to buy a Rolls Royce, a Cadillac and a Ferrari.

The sheik pressed his son further and after some thought the son said the final thing he wanted was a cowboy outfit.

'That's simple,' said the sheik, 'I'll buy the . . . police force!'

A constable brought a man into the police station for battery.

The station sergeant instructed him to put the man into a dry cell and to charge him in the morning.

*         *         *

A man appeared at the Crown Court on charges of murdering both his parents. His counsel pleaded on his behalf that he should be given a second chance because he was an orphan.

*         *         *

It was reported that some years ago Picasso was robbed in Paris. He was taken to the gendarmerie headquarters where he drew pictures of his assailants.

Shortly afterwards gendarmes arrested a taxi, a boat on the River Seine and the Eiffel Tower.

*         *         *

A man and his wife had just returned from a holiday in Majorca when the husband collapsed and died. The wife sent for the police.

A young constable arrived and looked at the body lying on the floor. He said to the wife: 'He's very tanned isn't he?'

The wife replied: 'Oh yes, I think his holiday did him good!'

*         *         *

The man standing on the scaffold, the condemned man, burst into a fit of uncontrollable laughter. The governor told him to control himself because it would make the circumstances harder for everyone concerned.

'Obviously, you don't understand,' said the prisoner still laughing, 'you're hanging the wrong man!'

*         *         *

A man took the occupants of the adjoining semi-detached house to court for being a public nuisance.

He complained that they constantly banged on the wall between the houses; they did it at all time of the day and the night.

The magistrates asked him if it kept him awake.

'Oh no,' was the reply, 'but it certainly puts me off my trumpet practice.'

*         *         *

A target criminal, much wanted by Scotland Yard, had evaded them for months. There was a suggestion that he had made his way to Ireland. The Yard sent to the Garda a very full description of the criminal including his previous convictions, his fingerprints and the photographs taken on the occasion of his last conviction. These photographs were of the usual format, one full-face and one of each profile.

Several weeks passed then a Telex was received from Dublin in the following terms: 'With reference to your dossier of 12th September, we are pleased to report that we have caught the men on the right and on the left but, so far, have not traced the man in the middle.'

         ★        ★        ★

The law is the true embodiment
Of everything that's excellent.
It has no kind of fault or flaw,
And I, my Lords, embody the law.

*Iolanthe—W. S. Gilbert*

         ★        ★        ★

It was the M1 and the sports car was travelling at a very excessive speed. A police patrol fitted in behind him and 'clocked' the speed at 140mph. Eventually the sports car was directed on to the hard-shoulder.

'Was I driving too fast?' said the driver.

'No sir,' said the constable, 'you were flying too low.'

         ★        ★        ★

A constable was walking down the street when a 'bus passed him at 30 mph. It had only travelled a few more yards when it came screeching to a halt for no apparent reason.

The constable went to it and found all the passengers and the conductor in a heap towards the front of the bus. He asked what had happened and the conductor explained that he had been collecting fares at the front of the bus and he had seen that a passenger wanted to get off at the next stop. Instead of ringing the bell he had tapped on the driver's window and the driver had 'slapped-on' everything he had.

At that moment the driver came around and, looking at the conductor, said: 'Never do that again!'

'Why?' asked the conductor.

'My last job,' explained the driver, 'was driving a hearse!'

The following is an extract from a chief superintendent's annual appraisal:

'Men will follow this officer—if only out of sheer curiosity.'

\*          \*          \*

A professor was on his first visit to Salford University when he lost his way in south Manchester. He stopped and asked an elderly policeman:

'How do I get to Salford University, please?'

'Young man,' the constable replied, 'you have to work very hard.'

\*          \*          \*

A certain Under Secretary at the Home Office was on a cross country tour of remand homes, and she was in a hurry. She was picked up at Exeter station by a police car and as her third visit took her to Plymouth, which then had its own police force, she was met and accompanied by the chief constable.

The remand home was a converted Victorian mansion with a semi-circular drive, and as they drew up some 30 young girls were avidly watching through the french windows. Seeing two gleaming black police cars, two police drivers, a chief constable and one female, one girl was heard to remark in awesome tones: 'Cor blimey, she must be a hot one. Two police cars and three cops to bring her in!'

\*          \*          \*

Two superintendents decided to have a day out at the sea. They spent their time looking at the sights and mid-afternoon found them on the cliffs overlooking the bay. Nearby was a convent and a stable which hired out donkeys for riding. For a giggle the two decided to hire out the two best looking donkeys. The owner explained that these two donkeys were normally reserved for nuns from the convent but were not needed for that purpose that day. He went on to tell them that they had been trained to answer very special words of command. They started at the words 'Good God' and stopped for 'Amen'.

Having started them the two superintendents enjoyed their ride and the donkeys managed a fair pace towards the edge of the cliffs. Struggling for the right word, one of the superintendents was able to stop his donkey, right on the edge of the cliff, with the command: 'Amen'.

On looking over the edge he could not avoid saying: 'Good God!'

A constable was walking down a street when he saw a drunk hammering on a door. As the constable approached the drunk asked him: 'Officer, is this the headquarters of Alcoholics Anonymous?'
'Yes, sir,' replied the constable, do you want to join?'
'No,' came the reply, 'I want to resign.'

*       *       *

The local football team was having a bad time. One saturday while the match was in progress a policeman saw two men climbing over the wall surrounding the ground. He shouted to them: You've paid to see them now climb right back in again and watch them.'

*       *       *

They called him necessity because he knew no law.

*       *       *

A ship was cruising in the South Pacific when it sank with the loss of everyone except a solicitor, a doctor and a vicar. After several hours in the water they came across an empty raft and climbed in. There was no food or water. The days passed and they realised that if they did not get food or water they would shortly die.

The following morning at dawn the doctor woke the others to point out that there was land on the horizon, but that there was a coral reef between the boat and land.

They agreed that one should swim ashore to attempt to obtain help. In the end it was agreed that, because he was the best swimmer, the solicitor should go.

Before he dived in the vicar led them in prayer for the solicitor's safe swim to shore. The solicitor then dived in and the other two watched his progress as he swam towards the reef. He had only been swimming for a couple of hundred yards when sharks were to be seen approaching him from all sides. The two in the boat looked on in terror but at the last moment each shark veered away and swam off.

'What a wonderful thing is the power of prayer,' said the vicar to the doctor.

'Prayer, nothing,' replied the doctor, 'what you have just seen is professional respect.'

Shortly after noon on a Saturday a constable was passing the Registry Office when he noticed a young couple who seemed rather upset. He went over to them and asked if there was anything he could do for them. The young man explained that he and his fiancée were to have been married at 11.45am but the taxi had let them down and went on to ask what time the office opened in the afternoon.

The constable had to explain to the couple that in fact the office was closed for the rest of the weekend.

The young lady was even more distraught and went on to explain that they were to leave that afternoon for a weekends honeymoon and now they hadn't got a marriage certificate.

'I'm sorry,' replied the constable, 'there is nothing that can be done about it until Monday at 9.00am.'

'Can't you even arrange for a cover-note for us,' pleaded the young man.

*   *   *

Police motor patrol stops a car which is exceeding the speed limit.

Driver: 'I'm sorry, officer, but you see I have an important appointment with my solicitor and I musn't be late.'

Constable: 'Quite right, sir, particularly now that you have another matter to discuss with him!'

*   *   *

A constable was standing opposite a public house shortly after closing time one night when the customers began to leave in one noisy, drunken mob. The majority of them made their way haltingly to the car park at the side. It was obvious that the majority were the worse for drink, but one man seemed far worse than the rest. He staggered from side to side, dropped his scarf; he was singing in a boisterous manner and kept falling to his knees. He, too, made his way to the car park, staggering into the path of the other cars as they all drove off. The constable kept a close eye on this man. As the drunk got to a car he fumbled for his keys, eventually found them, dropped them, picked them up and, with great deliberation, managed to open the car door. He climbed in, started the engine and drove out of the car park where the constable was waiting for him on the road outside.

The constable held up his hand and the car stopped. He asked the driver to get out, which he did.

'I suspect that you are under the influence of alcohol,' said the constable.

'I think not,' replied the driver in a perfectly modulated and steady voice, 'I am completely teetotal. The only drink I have had tonight was a single orange juice.'

It was perfectly obvious to the constable that this man was absolutely sober.

'Can I have your name?' he asked.

'Frank Jones.'

'How old are you Mr Jones?'

'Forty-five.'

'Where do you live?'

'55 Acacia Avenue.'

'And what is your occupation?'

'I am a professional decoy!'

*          *          *

One of Her Majesty's Inspectors of Constabulary was inspecting a certain police force. He asked the chief constable if there had been any innovations since his last inspection. The chief constable replied that he had started a vice squad, a drug squad and a serious crime squad. The inspector asked: 'Have you a murder squad?' and the the chief constable replied: 'Who do you want murdering?'

*          *          *

A man had worked all his life for a farmer making deliveries in the farmer's lorry to places within a few miles of the farm in North Yorkshire. It was an isolated rural area and the driver never strayed very far from his home or the farm. He never took holidays and his only interest was his pint of mild in the 'Ploughman' every night of the year. He turned up for work one morning at his usual time and the farmer told him that he wanted him to take a load of 'spuds' to an address in London.

Fred, who couldn't read, was not an argumentative person so he said: 'Yes boss,' and commenced to load the lorry. He had finished this by seven a.m. so he climbed into the cab and drove off. Eventually he found himself on the A1. He had been travelling some miles watching the signposts go by when he decided to turn off. He went a mile or two and then, seeing a cyclist, stopped.

'Is this London?' he asked.

'No,' replied the cyclist, 'this is Doncaster.'

Fred climbed back into the lorry, turned it round and eventually found himself travelling south once more along the A1. He travelled for what seemed to him to be an eternity until he decided to turn off at another junction. Again he asked if it was London when he came to a large town. The answer came back: 'No, this is Grantham.'

Back on the A1 he progressed until he found himself travelling mile after mile in a built-up area. The traffic became denser and denser until it was nose to tail.

Eventually he found himself on a bridge and saw a policeman walking towards him. He leaned out of the passenger window and asked: 'I say is this London?'

The constable replied: 'Yes sir, this is London.'

'Right then,' said Fred, 'where do you want me to drop these 'ere spuds off?'

★      ★      ★

In the modern police service of today there is a need for both experts and good all-rounders. Perhaps the two should be defined:

An Expert: One who knows more and more about less and less until eventually he knows everything about nothing.

A Good All-Rounder: One who knows less and less about more and more until eventually he knows about everything.

★      ★      ★

In the local newspaper it was reported that several criminals had been arrested by Constable Jack Timms, a defective in the police force. Obviously the constable was rather annoyed so he rang the editor and asked for a correction in the following weeks issue. In this edition the apology appeared in the following form: 'We wish to apologize to Constable Timms, he is not a defective in the police force, in fact he is a detective in the police farce.'

★      ★      ★

Walking through a graveyard one night a constable noticed that a hole had appeared in one of the graves. He made his way to the gatehouse and told the keeper who returned to the graveside with him.

He looked down into the hole and said: 'Oh yes, that's old Mozart.'

The constable asked: 'What's he doing there?'

'Decomposing,' came the reply.

A man was mistakenly arrested for an attack on an attractive young woman. He could not have committed the offence for he was many miles away at the time: apart from this he had two thoroughly trustworthy witnesses. Neverthless the woman positively identified him, and he was charged.

He appeared before the magistrates and the charges were read to him and he was asked to plead. He pleaded guilty and was sentenced to a term of six months imprisonment suspended for two years.

As he left court he was approached by his two witnesses who were still showing amazement.

One asked: 'Why on earth did you plead guilty when we could have proved conclusively that you couldn't have possible committed the offences?'

Man: 'Well, when I heard of all the things I was supposed to have done I was so proud I couldn't resist pleading guilty!'

⋆          ⋆          ⋆

A policeman was surprised to see a man at a 'bus stop with an alligator on a lead.

Policeman: 'Are you taking it to the zoo then?'

Man: 'No, I am taking it to the cinema—we went to the zoo yesterday.'

⋆          ⋆          ⋆

A jury is a group of people of average ignorance.

⋆          ⋆          ⋆

Copper Nitrate: What a constable receives for working the night relief?

⋆          ⋆          ⋆

The judge had heard the early part of the case in the Crown Court but as the evidence was given he made the decision that the rest of the case should be heard 'in camera'.

The defendant objected on the grounds that he didn't know the meaning of the expression 'in camera', but the judge overruled the objection, saying, 'I know what it means, the prosecution knows what it means, the defending counsel knows what it means, and the jury knows what it means. Now clear the court.'

When this was done, counsel for the defendant asked the defendant to tell the court, in his own words, what had happened on the night in question.

'Well,' he said, 'I was walking this girl home along a country lane, and we decided to take a short cut across a field. Halfway across the field, she seemed tired, so we sat down for a rest. It was a nice summer's night and I felt a bit romantic so I gave her a kiss. She gave me a kiss. I gave her a kiss. She gave me a kiss. Then, 10 minutes later, hi-tiddly-hi-ti!'

The judge said: 'Hi-tiddly-hi-ti?—what on earth does that mean?'

'Well,' answered the defendant. 'The defending counsel knows what it means . . . the prosecuting counsel knows what it means and the jury knows what it means! . . . and if you'd been there with your camera, *you'd* know what it means!'

*       *       *

A man arrested for murder managed to have a word with one of the jurors, and offered him one thousand pounds if he could persuade his fellow jurors to reduce the charge to one of manslaughter.

The jury was out for three days and eventually returned a verdict of manslaughter. The prisoner ran over to his 'friend' on the jury and before the warders had a chance to restrain him, he said: 'Thanks, was it difficult?'

'Yes,' replied the juror, 'the rest of them wanted to acquit you.'

*       *       *

A young doctor joined his first practice and one of the senior members thought that it would be beneficial if he took the young chap on his rounds with him.

They called at the first house and were taken upstairs to where a rather obese lady was lying in bed. After the usual preliminaries the older doctor took out his thermometer. He shook it and in doing so dropped it. He bent down and picked it up and then took the woman's temperature. This completed he said to the woman: 'Much the same, but you won't fully recover until you give up eating chocolate.' With that he and the young doctor left the house.

Once outside the young doctor said: 'That was a quick diagnosis, how did you know from taking her temperature that she was eating chocolate?'

'Easy,' replied the elder partner, 'when I dropped the thermometer I looked under the bed and saw a two pound box of chocolates.'

At the next call it was decided that the young doctor should carry out the examination.

Once more they were taken upstairs to the bedroom but this time lying in the bed was a most attractive young woman. The young doctor was more than keen to use his stethoscope but his hands were shaking too much. He took out his thermometer, shook it and dropped it on the floor. He picked it up and tested the young lady's temperature. This done he said: 'Nothing serious, but for the time being don't get too involved with the police.' With that the two doctors left the house. Once outside the older doctor asked: 'What sort of advice was that you gave?' The young doctor replied: 'I learned a little from you; when I picked up the thermometer I too looked under the bed—there was a police sergeant.'

*      *      *

A policeman found a boy of about seven crying at a street corner.

Constable: 'Now what's wrong with you laddie?'

Boy: 'It's my birthday.'

Constable: 'Haven't you had any presents?'

Boy (crying even more): 'Yes, I've had dozens of lovely presents.'

Constable: 'Well aren't you having a party then?'

Boy: 'Oh yes, my mum's made a lot of cakes, jellies and trifles and all my friends are coming round and we are going to play games.'

Constable: 'Why are you crying then?'

Boy: 'I'm lost!'

*      *      *

An Englishman, a Scot and an Irishman found themselves in a South American country. Being short of money they decided to rob a bank. During the robbery a cashier was shot and shortly afterwards the three were arrested by the police. Eventually they were tried, found guilty and sentenced to death by shooting.

On the appointed day they were taken one by one from their cell. Firstly the Englishman was taken out and placed against the wall. As the firing squad raised their rifles, he suddenly shouted 'Avalanche!' at the top of his voice. The soldiers in panic, threw down their arms and ran. Taking advantage of this, the Englishman ran out of the gate and escaped.

Having seen this from the window of the cell when it was his turn the Scot shouted 'Flood!', with the same success as the Englishman.

The Irishman was determined to do exactly the same. As the rifles were pointed towards him he carefully chose his time and shouted 'Fire!'

*          *          *

Lord Birkett in an after-dinner speech:
'Gentlemen, the speech you are about to hear I have delivered twice before, once to the Bar Council and once to the inmates of Dartmoor Prison. I would ask any of you who were present on either occasion to bear with me.'

*          *          *

A salesman tired of his job joined the police force. A friend asked how he enjoyed his new job.

'The pay is good and the hours OK,' he replied, 'but best of all the customer is always wrong!'

*          *          *

A businessman who had consulted his solicitor for some legal advice ran into an acquaintance to whom he recounted his experiences. 'Why spend money on a lawyer?' the friend asked, 'didn't you see all those law books while you sat in his office? Well the answers were all there. What he told you, you could have easily have read yourself in those very big tomes and you would have avoided paying a big fee.'

'Yes that's all very true. The only difference is that the lawyer knows what page it is on!'

*          *          *

Prisoner at the bar: 'As God is my Judge, my Lord, I am not guilty.'
Judge: 'He's not, I am, you are—six months.'

*          *          *

Barrister representing the prisoner: 'I must apologise, my Lord, I appear to be running out of time.'
Judge: 'Mr Lawrence, you ran out of time an hour ago, you are now in danger of trespassing on Eternity.'

*          *          *

**Spike Milligan**
Policeman to prisoner: 'Are you going to come quietly or have I got to wear ear-plugs?'

A vicar attending a conference of clergymen left his car in a no waiting area with a note under his windscreen wiper: 'I am a minister of religion attending a conference which I have done for 15 years. I am already late and the parking places are getting fewer and fewer—*forgive us our trespasses.*'

When he returned to the car some time later he found another note: 'I am an officer of the law and I have been on this beat for 20 years. My superior is due within the hour and things are getting stricter—*lead us not into temptation.*'

\*          \*          \*

The punishment for bigamy—two mothers-in-law.

\*          \*          \*

Constables and sergeants sweat.
Inspectors and chief inspectors perspire.
Superintendents and above simply glow.

\*          \*          \*

'My Lord,' said the prisoner, 'I don't know what to do.'
'Why, what is the matter?' asked the judge.
'I swore to tell the truth, but every time I try some lawyer objects.'

\*          \*          \*

A coach party left Yorkshire for the Rugby League Cup Final—for all of them it was their first visit to London. After the match they made their separate ways back to the coach after having become parted in the West End. Joe Murgatroyd felt lost without his bosom pal Tom Ramsbottam and, seeing a constable, went up to him. 'Excuse me, constable, have you seen Tom Ramsbottam?' 'Sorry sir,' replied the constable, 'I'm afraid I don't know him and there's a lot of people in London.' Joe: 'Aye, I know there is, there's a trip in from Pudsey!'

\*          \*          \*

He said that he had enjoyed infancy so much he was really looking forward to adultery!

\*          \*          \*

What did the thief give his wife at Christmas? A furry stole!

\*          \*          \*

New Scotland Yard was broken into last night and all the toilets were stolen. A police spokesman said: 'At this moment we have nothing to go on.'

Three Irishmen in America broke into Fort Knox and stole the lead off the roof.

*         *         *

A constable on motor patrol told an Irish lorry driver that he should dip his headlights, so Paddy went and drove his lorry into a nearby lake.

*         *         *

A traffic warden has been described as a wasp with a £10 sting!

*         *         *

An advertisement was placed in the local newspaper for a handyman at the local 'nick'. Several applications were received and eventually some of the applicants were called for interview by the divisional commander and his chief clerk.

The first man was shown in and the commander asked him if he had had any previous experience. The man replied: 'No.' He was then asked if he could carry out small repair jobs. The answer was: 'No.' The next question was 'Can you change light bulbs?' Again: 'No.' The interviewers asked several other questions from which they deduced that the man was hopeless.

The divisional commander, rather annoyed, said: 'The advertisement stated that we want a handyman, you appear useless, why did you apply for the job as handyman?' 'I live just around the corner,' came the reply.

*         *         *

Magistrate: 'Did you or did you not strike the policeman?'
Prisoner: 'The answer is in the infirmary.'

*         *         *

On a busy street corner a constable on traffic control saw an old lady beckoning him over. He held up a stream of cars, buses, trucks and taxis. He walked over to her and asked if he could help. Putting her hand on his arm she said in a soft voice: 'Oh no thank you officer, I just wanted to tell you that your number is the same as the number of my favourite hymn!'

*         *         *

The chief constable had been retired for many years. Each year he was invited by the President of the Senior Officers' Mess to attend the annual re-union. Steadfastly over the years he refused, despite attempts by his wife to get him to attend. Eventually, however, his wife's persuasion won him round and he very reluctantly agreed to go. On the night a car was sent for him and he went.

It was after midnight when he returned and his wife was eagerly awaiting him.

'Did you enjoy yourself?' was her first question.

'Not at all' was the reply. 'There was an assistant chief constable complaining about his liver trouble, a chief superintendent about his kidneys and a chief constable wouldn't stop talking about his heart complaint.'

'Well was it a good re-union?' asked his wife.

'It wasn't a re-union,' he replied, 'it was more like an organ recital.'

\*         \*         \*

The commandant of the cadets training school had introduced religious education as an addition to the school syllabus.

Her Majesty's Inspector of Constabulary came on his annual inspection and, at his request, toured the training school. He was pleased to hear of the introduction of religious education and asked one of the cadets, Barry Jones 'Who knocked down the Walls of Jericho?' Jones replied immediately: 'I'm sorry sir, but it wasn't me.'

HMI was amazed at this complete show of ignorance and mentioned it to the chief constable at the end of the inspection. The chief constable said: 'I know Jones, a great lad with a promising future. If he says that it wasn't him I am sure that it wasn't him.'

Not satisfied HMI wrote a letter to the Home Office pointing out what had transpired.

In due course he received the following reply: Dear Sir, with reference to your letter of 25th ultimo concerning the Walls of Jericho, this is a matter for the Department of the Environment to whom I have forwarded your letter.

\*         \*         \*

The value of speech is often in inverse ratio to its length—the shorter the better!

A good example is a speech made by defence counsel in an American murder trial.

'Gentlemen of the jury. If you convict my client she will be taken from here to a cold damp cell in Sing Sing prison. There all of her lovely blonde hair will be shaved off, she will be strapped to a chair and burnt to a cinder. But, gentlemen, if you acquit her, she will return to her luxurious apartment, the telephone number of which is . . .'

*          *          *

The solicitor had a very stubborn client. Despite very firm advice to settle the case the client flatly refused. 'I'll take it to every court in the land. If I don't win I'll take it to the Appeal Court and if necessary to the House of Lords. If that doesn't work I'll even go to E.R. herself!'

'You mean Her Majesty the Queen?'

'No, Esther Rantzen.'

*          *          *

'Please give me your money and any valuables you may have with you,' said the hold-up man politely.

'Why should I?' asked the intended victim, 'I'm giving nothing away to an Irishman without a fight.'

'How did you know I was Irish?'

'You've sawn off the wrong end of the shotgun!'

*          *          *

'Please give me all your money,' pleaded the beggar, 'all I have in this world is this gun.'

*          *          *

One crafty villain taught himself to crack safes with his feet. It drove the fingerprint men around the bend!

*          *          *

Two sergeants were talking together. 'I'm a man of principles,' said the first, for example, I never slept with my wife until after we were married; I wonder whether you can say as much?'

'Let me see,' was the reply, 'remind me, what was your wife's name?'

*          *          *

A long-distance lorry driver went into a transport cafe and ordered sausage and chips, and a cup of tea. As he sat down to eat his meal, three motor cycles drove into the car park outside. The owners were greasers on their way to some 'aggro' at the seaside. They entered the cafe and, unfastening their leather jackets, approached the lorry driver's table. One ate his sausages, another ate his chips and the third drank his tea.

Without saying a word, the lorry driver left the cafe, got into his lorry and drove off.

The leader of the 'greasers' laughed and said: 'He wasn't much of a man was he?'

'Not much of a driver either,' said the cafe owner, 'he's just driven his lorry over three motor-bikes.'

*     *     *

There was the chief constable who thought he was an excellent after-dinner speaker. One day he dreamt he was making a speech and woke up to find that he was!

*     *     *

The majority of police officers take an interest in sport and in recent years have become involved in what might be termed as the more adventurous sports.

One constable became involved in free-fall parachute jumping. He joined a local club and attended several evenings to learn the theory and take part in some of the 'ground' practice. Several weeks passed and his instructor thought it time for his first jump.

The following Sunday morning he reported to the airfield with several others. The instructor gave them a further period of instruction and then took them to a nearby plane. They all boarded and the plane took off.

When the appropriate height had been reached they jumped in turn. The constable was the last. As he fell he counted and then pulled the cord; nothing happened. He pulled again, still nothing. He made several attempts but to no avail. The ground was getting nearer and nearer and then he saw a man coming up towards him on a gas cooker.

He shouted to him: 'I say, mate, do you know how to open parachutes?'

The man replied: 'No, do you know how to repair gas leaks?'

*     *     *

The chief inspector was something of a bore; he was a notorious name dropper. No matter how famous a person might be if that person was mentioned the chief inspector would say that he knew him or her very well. This manner so infuriated a fellow chief inspector that the latter challenged the other. He said that he would lay a bet of £1,000 that the braggart could not prove he knew three famous people. The bet was accepted.

It was agreed that one famous person would be English, another American and the third Italian. They managed to arrange a period of leave together and set off, firstly, to London. On arrival they went straight to Downing Street. Chief Inspector Brown, the know-all, asked his challenger, Chief Inspector Jones to wait outside No. 10. He then went up to the door, had a word with the constable on duty and was immediately let in. About half-an-hour passed before the door opened and out stepped Brown closely followed by the Prime Minister—it was obvious that he was well-known and well-received.

They next went to Washington in the United States. There they took a taxi to the White House. Much the same happened, Brown was given VIP treatment and was entertained by the President.

The third leg of the journey was to Rome. This time they headed for St Peter's Square. Once there Brown said to Jones, 'I've won two-thirds of the bet I'm now going to finalise it by proving I'm well-known to the Pope. I want you to wait here and watch that balcony in the Vatican.'

With that he left and went into the main entrance of the Vatican. Time passed and St. Peter's Square was almost packed to capacity. After two hours there was movement at the back of the balcony and out walked Chief Inspector Brown followed by the Pope. Jones was completely taken aback and only just heard a voice behind him asking a friend:

'I wonder who that is with Chief Inspector Brown?'

*        *        *

The chief constable lived in a house on the outskirts of the city together with his wife, his aged mother and their pet cat. As a family they were devoted to the cat. His mother had been ill for some time but fortunately recovered sufficiently for he and his wife to take a holiday they had arranged some months previously, in Greece.

The day of departure arrived and the chief's driver took them to the airport. The chief had arranged for the driver to make daily calls at his house during the time they were away.

Two weeks passed and, bronzed, the chief and his wife returned to be met at the airport by the driver.

When the luggage had been loaded into the boot and they had commenced the journey home the chief asked how the cat had been during their absence. The driver replied: 'I'm sorry, sir, but your cat died the day after you left.'

The chief constable was obviously distressed as was his wife, they had loved the cat. He was rather annoyed by the blunt way the driver had passed on the awful information and said to him: 'When you have bad news to impart you should introduce it gently; in reply to my question you should have said something like: The day after you left the cat got on to the roof and was playing with a ball when it slipped, and fell into the path of a lorry. We thought it was alright until a few days later it passed peacefully away.'

Silence reigned for a few more miles before the chief constable spoke again: 'Incidentally, how is my mother?' Replied the driver: 'Well you see, sir, on the day you left she got on to the roof . . .'

*        *        *

Notice on the wall of the chief constable's office: 'To err is human, to forgive is not the policy in this police force.'

*        *        *

# TRUE STORIES

During my years of research into humour within the police service I have repeatedly come across variations on a theme—the story would contain the same basic elements but differed on locality and personalities. Some others might be termed as being apocryphal but as near as I can determine the stories in this section can be classified as true.

### Marti Caine, comedienne and singer

Trevor Howard was filming 'Witchhunter General' a film about Cromwell. The crew were doing nightshots on location a few miles from the studio. Mr Howard decided to go to the location on his motor cycle rather than in the company coach, for the night was clear and fine. Off he went in full 'gear' for the part (red tights, velvet knickerbockers, armoured breast plate, helmet, gauntlet, boots and sword) when he felt, rather than saw, the boys in blue in a patrol car behind him. After a mile or so they flagged him down. A very serious looking constable went over to him, held out a breathalyser and said: 'Good evening, Sir. I wonder if you would mind holding this while I blow into it?'

\*      \*      \*

### Mike Yarwood, television personality, comedian, impersonator

I was going a little too fast along a road in Surrey, a nice, wide carriageway, and may I say in my own defence, it's easily done. This time I was driving and was flagged down by a police car. Out got a sergeant and a very keen constable, who looked as though he was dying to make his first arrest. Over they came. Fortunately the more senior of the two was a fan and chatted to me for quite a few minutes about recent television shows which he had enjoyed (making me even later for rehearsals, but I was in no position to complain).

'I love the way you take the mickey out of Harold,' he said. All this time the young constable's face was getting more and more angry—if he had had his way, I would have had a ticket. I could tell that. However, the sergeant sent me on my way saying: 'Well keep on doing Harold and, by the way, watch your speed, won't you?'

**Shaw Taylor, television personality and presenter of 'Police Five'**
Some while ago a rather large, villainous looking character
came up to me in the street and said: "ere you're that bloke what
does Police Five ain't you?' As he looked somewhat menacing I
made a quick mental note of the best way to run once I'd ducked
under his rather ham-like fist.

'Yes, I am,' I said, preparing for the quick getaway. But it
wasn't necessary. 'You could de me a favour,' said the big man.
'Where's all that bleeding Gordons gin you 'ad on last week
gone to? I said to the wife, that's nice, that should be through
this week, and we 'aven't 'ad a smell of it. We've had J&B scotch
and the Bristol sherry but we 'aven't 'ad a drop of that gin. Some
so and so's doing me down—if you can find out who it is I'll see
you right!!'

I pointed out that he'd rather got the wrong angle on the
programme—that it wasn't an advertising magazine for the
week's best buy—but it didn't seem to sink in.

*       *       *

The setting up of cameras to film 'Police Five' always attracts an
interested crowd of bystanders. On a recent robbery at a
jeweller's shop we had just finished filming when an elderly lady
inquired 'What are you doing?' I explained. 'Oh yes,' she said,
'that robbery, I know who did that.' I thought I had misheard.
'What did you say?' I asked. 'I know who did it' she repeated
'they're two very naughty boys.'

I called the detective across—'I think this lady might have
some information for you' I informed him, and got on with
wrapping up the shooting. A few minutes later an incredulous
detective said to me: 'You know that old darling has just given
me two names of what she calls naughty boys—I've checked
them out with records and they're two right villains. I'll lay a
pound to a penny this one's down to them.' 'Great,' I said, 'but
don't you go rushing off to arrest them before 'Police Five' goes
out—I've got a programme to worry about.' 'No problem,' said
the detective, 'I've got their address—I'll let them watch the
programme first!'

And so it was that two 'naughty boys' sat watching 'Police
Five' chortling over the fact that their job was on the
programme. Hardly had the credits faded before there was a
knock on the door. 'Good evening, we are police officers and we

have reason to believe . . .' And today, serving their time in a well known prison, are two 'naughty lads' who are still amazed at the rapid results achieved by 'Police Five'!!!

*        *        *

### Paul Daniels, TV comedian and magician

At the time this incident happened, I was having a house altered in the Kensington area, and the builders who were doing the alterations were anxious to have a skip delivered to take away their building rubble. Unfortunately, in the days prior to the skip arriving a Jaguar broke down and was left in the residents' only parking area slap bang outside my house. The occupants of the car took away the seats, and I took this to be a gesture that the car had been dumped. Having just performed at several police charities, I decided to use the power of being a Star and a Do-gooder together, to get the police to remove the offending vehicle. A telephone call to the local constabulary and they promised that they would send round a man immediately.

Two policemen turned up and looked at the car for a long time. I knew that looking at it wouldn't shift it, so I went out to talk to them. At that time I was working in the West End of London at the Prince of Wales Theatre where cars are being towed away nightly when they were parked in seemingly very inoffensive places and for no reason at all. So, it was only natural that I would assume that this was a copper's hobby. 'No,' they said, 'the West End is a different area, we can't tow it away from here.'

'Why not?' says I. 'It isn't taxed, it is parked in a residents' parking zone without the proper permission displayed in the windscreen, and it is a nuisance that is delaying my alterations.' 'Sorry,' says they, 'but as it is not causing an obstruction there is nothing we can do.' And of they jolly well went.

I gave a nod to the builder after they had gone to put the bumper of his lorry up the back end of the Jaguar, and he pushed it out of the way right up on to the corner of the road. Now I will get this eyesore shifted I thought, and phoned the local constabulary again to inform them of the obstruction.

No sooner the call made, and within minutes a van full of policemen arrived. The builders and I watched to see how they would drive the Jaguar away, considering it had no seats inside.

The burly officers of the law leapt from their trusty steed and pushed the damn thing back again—got in their van and drove off!!!

(*Editor's note:* 'I like it, not a lot . . .')

\*        \*        \*

## Alan Melville, television and radio scriptwriter

My relations with the police, up to now, have always been extremely cordial; never more so than fairly early one Sunday morning a few years ago. I was doing a weekly TV show at the time and we did our final rehearsal and recording each Sunday starting at 10.00am. Well you know what it is about Sunday mornings . . . I admit I slept in a bit, and then I had to check my pools, and the car needed filling up with petrol, and what with one thing and another I didn't leave Brighton until around 8.50am.

It was an absolutely gorgeous morning, there was hardly any traffic on the roads, and—well, I know anything I may say may be taken down and used in evidence against me—but I fairly belted along. I was astonished just after leaving the Sutton by-pass when I was overtaken by another car. I was even more astonished when I was waved down in what seemed to me a somewhat high-handed manner. Out of the other car stepped a very young constable—they say the police force looks younger the older you get, and this guy made me feel positively Methuselah. He was extremely polite, had a charming smile—the following dialogue ensued:

Constable: 'Morning, sir.'

Me: 'Er—good morning.'

Constable: 'Lovely morning, sir.'

Me: 'Beautiful, isn't it?'

Constable: 'Got a speedometer?'

Me: 'Oh, yes.'

Constable: 'Working is it?'

Me: 'Er—I think so, yes.'

Constable: 'Accurate?'

Me: 'I wouldn't know about that, officer. It registers a higher speed the faster one goes, if that's what you mean.'

Constable: 'You know it's been very interesting, sir. You were doing 63 through Crawley, then you got up to 78 a bit later on, then you seemed to lose interest a bit sir. I mean, you were down to only around 50 going through that narrow viaduct thing in Reigate. However, you didn't half perk up along the Sutton by-pass. Ninety-one we made it.'

Me: *(beginning to wimper)* 'Well, officer. I'll be perfectly frank. I've cut things a bit fine this morning. I'm supposed to be at Shepherd's Bush in about 12 minutes—and you must admit there's hardly any traffic on the road, and I don't think I was in any way driving without due care and attention. I'm doing a television series, you see, and the producer gets awfully cross if we're late for rehearsal.'

Constable: 'Oh, you're one of those, are you?'

Me: 'Er, yes.'

LONG PAUSE

Constable: 'All right, then, clear off.'

⋆　　⋆　　⋆

**Lt. Colonel R. D. Ashworth, Military Tutor, Home Defence College**

I was travelling in my car to lecture a class of police officers on Home Defence at 'Tally Ho', the West Midlands Police Training Centre. I had the car radio switched on and I heard a doctor saying how he had found that fashions in men's underwear were changing dramatically. He related a story of a 6'6" burly police sergeant who had been to his surgery. The doctor had asked the sergeant to drop his trousers. The sergeant had done this and revealed a natty pair of pink Y-fronts emblazoned with the legend 'Who's a cheeky boy?'

When I arrived at the Training School and stood in front of a class of police officers, all of whom seemed in excess of 6'6" in height, I related the story. About half the class laughed but a good half remained in stony silence which made me wonder what type of underwear they sported.

When I returned to the Home Defence College I told this to the police superintendent staff tutor . . . *he* didn't laugh!

⋆　　⋆　　⋆

**Denis Norden, broadcaster, writer & raconteur**

A high point of hilarity I can remember sharing with the police force occurred when I reported to a station sergeant the theft of the car that I'd hired after my own car had been stolen.

**John Timpson, television and radio presenter**
On the 'Today' programme on Radio Four we used to get a
spate of 'ho-ho' misprints and touches of humour. Following
are two examples:

'Daily Telegraph' report about a distinguished lady
magistrate 'Fifteen years as a magistrate at Bow Street dealing
with prostitutes and at Great Marlborough Street—*mainly
shoplifting from big stores*—have brought her a wardrobe of
plain navy and black dresses suitable for the bench.'

\*          \*          \*

Mrs Mary Whitehouse on a pornography case: 'All those who
are exploiting bona fide sex education to make porn and cash
must see the red light . . .'

\*          \*          \*

**Roger Moore, the 'Saint'**
The height of fame! I had already been under contract for two
years at MGM in Hollywood and came back to England for a
holiday. I parked my car outside a pub in Leicester Square for a
quick jar with a couple of old friends and 10 minutes later I
came out to find a police officer standing over my car in a very
ugly mood indeed.

He demanded to see my driving licence and then said:
'Moore? Are you George Moore's son from Bow Street?' I said I
was and with that he smiled kindly on my parking offence. Not
because I was Roger Moore, the up-and-coming actor, but the
son of George Moore the policeman from Bow Street.

\*          \*          \*

A detective sergeant in Brighton was in the CID office when a
man came in to report that his wallet had been stolen at
Brighton Railway Station. The circumstances were that the
complainant had travelled by train from Victoria Railway
Station in London and on arrival at Brighton had, for obvious
reasons, made his way to the gents. He entered a cubicle and
with much haste took off his jacket which he placed on a hook
fixed to the back of the door. He had just managed to get seated
when a hand reached up over the door and, with a walking stick,
removed his jacket. Later when he was able to leave the cubicle
he found his jacket on the floor outside. His wallet containing
all his money was missing.

After explaining the facts the detective sergeant replied: 'Now

I know what they mean when they say—'he was caught with his trousers down'.'

The complainant was not amused!

*       *       *

**Harry Secombe, singer, comedian, goon**
I was driving along happily and singing 'Lady of Spain' which was being played on the car radio, when I heard a siren coming up behind me.

The policeman said: 'Wait until I tell them at the station that I've nicked Harry Secombe,' and then proceeded to book me for speeding.

The conversation which ensued—'You were exceeding the speed limit, Mr Secombe' . . . 'Yes, officer, and isn't it a lovely day for it?' . . .was duly reported at court. After signing the policeman's autograph book he went on his way—later I paid my £7 fine.

The most expensive autograph I've ever signed!

*       *       *

**Bob Warman, television presenter, ATV**
It was 'hats off' to the town drunk the day he hobbled into the dock on crutches. Only the previous week he'd been fined by the stipendiary magistrate with a final warning that the next time would definitely mean a prison sentence. The crutches looked like a master stroke. Placing them against the dock, the defendant leaned heavily on the rail and with every ounce of emotion he could summon, pleaded to the stipendiary not to send him down. 'Arthritis,' he whined, 'it's killing me. I can hardly walk. It'd be like sending a cripple away.'

The stipendiary listened in silence. It was in the defendant's favour that he was at last getting some treatment. The hospital that lent him the crutches must be offering a modicum of supervision. Perhaps then just this once . . . but this really was positively the last chance. The sigh of relief from the gallery turned to shouts of hilarity as the defendant, overcome with relief, headed for freedom. He turned at the door, a puzzled look on his face, trying to pinpoint the object of mirth. He followed a dozen gazes in the direction of the dock where, leaning against . . .

**Barry Took, presenter of 'Points of View', BBC TV**

Once, many years ago, I owned a Bentley S3 saloon, a car that caused me more anguish than any other I've owned. For a start I couldn't afford it (don't ask me why I bought it in the first place); passers-by would scratch their initials on it, and once, driving through a French seaside town, a small boy shouted 'capitaliste' at me—unnerving because I'm not. The climax came when I was making a documentary film in Holmfirth, Yorkshire.

We all, that's to say the director, camera crew, production assistant etc, stayed in the nearby town of H. (no names, no pack-drill), me in the Station Hotel, the crew in another hotel some hundred yards away. After shooting ended we'd pile into the Bentley and I'd take them all back to their hotel. One night they invited me in for a meal and a drink—I accepted, but leaving at about midnight, my hand was reaching for the door handle of the Bentley when several policemen emerged from the shadows.

'You're not thinking of driving that, are you?' said the sergeant.

'No,' I lied, 'just getting my script.' The sergeant laughed mirthlessly.

'Let me see your licence'—and so on.

It turned out that the 'hotel' I'd just left was notorious—well, I've forgotten the Yorkshire for house of ill-repute, but that's what it was, and the police, who'd been watching the place for some time, concluded, wrongly I assure you, that I was a customer. This was before the days of 'Points of View' and I was totally unknown—and to be fair must have looked suspicious. If you're out at midnight in H. it's assumed you're an early riser or up to no good.

The story doesn't have much of an ending. The police checked my documents and found everything in order except that the MOT test certificate was four days out of date. 'Get it fixed and report to the station tomorrow.' I was told.

So filming had to wait while I spent the next day in garage and police station. As I said to the director later, 'that's the last time I come home for supper with you!'

*       *       *

When a man's got to jog, he's got to jog.

This story concerns a fitness fanatic pounding the streets of Matlock, Bath in the early hours of the morning.

Inspector Golder and Constable Walters, the only other beings about at that time of the day, were sitting together in the inspector's car. This stood squarely on the jogger's intended route.

Not a pause. Not a change in pace. On and on came the jogger, on to the bonnet, over the roof, down the back, and off into the darkness. After the traditional exchange of 'What the !!!!!!' and '!!!! me,' the two officers sprinted after the runner.

The charge is not clear but the magistrate who subsequently fined him £15 remarked: 'We are not going to let the police force be overrun in this manner.'

\*        \*        \*

**Steve Jones, TV and radio personality**
Perhaps I could recount an incident which happened to me at our local police station. It's mildly amusing rather than hilarious, but true nevertheless, and shows the double power of television.

The Chiswick police had organised a painting competition 'The law in the year 2000'. It was for children of primary school age and both myself and John Thaw were asked to be judges.

As we entered the station a little old lady, who was obviously a fan of my programme and 'The Sweeney', stopped us and had a real go at me for not being the nice chap I appeared on TV. I couldn't understand what she meant until it dawned on me that she was seeing John Thaw as Regan and believed him to be arresting me for some criminal offence!

\*        \*        \*

**Extract from the Sunday Express**
The bank had been open for only about half an hour when the smartly-dressed man walked in, his tie straight, his dark suit brushed and well pressed.

He walked to one of the check-in tills and, in a strong Irish accent asked for ten 10 pence pieces for two 50p coins. The girl cashier obliged. The man then asked for details about opening a trust account at the bank—the Midland branch at Ewell, Surrey.

This was a new one on the girl, who had never heard of such a scheme. She sent him to the inquiry counter.

An hour or two later the man returned and went to a different counter, only with the same idea.

'Could I please have ten 10 pence pieces for two 50ps?' he asked.

Shortly after lunch the man reappeared and approached the girl he had seen on his visit. By this time he was getting used to the general layout of the place.

And this time he had a new idea. He produced two 10 pence pieces.

'Can I please have four five pence pieces for the phone?' he asked.

The girl, aware of the bank's reputation for helpfulness, turned to oblige.

But when she looked up her smile froze. The man had pulled a gun out of his coat and it was pointing at her.

'Give me the money,' he shouted in best popular bank raid fashion. But the girl ducked and ran.

That baffled the Irishman, who had not calculated on such a move. Left staring at an empty counter and still holding the gun, he turned and fled, leaving behind his two 10 pence pieces.

A bank spokesman said: 'We are 20 pence to the good. We will hold it for the man if he would care to return for it . . .'

*        *        *

A man parked his car in the car park of a London store to do some shopping. When he returned his car was missing so he dashed back into the store and telephoned the police.

On going back to the car park, to his astonishment there was his car. He drove away—but before he had travelled the length of the street, a police car with sirens blaring and lights flashing pulled in front of him.

Out jumped two policemen and, before he knew what was happening, he was in the back of the police car. When did he steal the car, why and where from?

It was only after five hours in the police station, and numerous phone calls, that the police finally released him, laughing heartily at his mistake.

Well, how was he to know the store had two car parks and he'd left by different doors each time?

**Eldon Griffiths, MP, adviser to Police Federation**
Gives particulars of three officers dismissed from the Met. in the
late 19th century:

*Constable 'A':* Dismissed the force. The charge—going round
knocking on doors in the hope of getting beer or spirits—and
far too often succeeding!

*Constable 'B':* Dismissed the force. The charge—found in bed
with a married woman, not his wife, with his boots on!

*Constable 'C':* Dismissed the force. The charge—discovered
on duty in a shop doorway after midnight, together with a loose
woman, with his LAMP out!

*　　　*　　　*

A man who found a credit card went to a store and tried to
obtain a suitcase was described as 'optimistic in the extreme' by
defending solicitor at West London Court.

John Joseph Tyson, 46, an Irish Painter, was given a three
months suspended sentence after admitting receiving the card,
forging a payments slip and attempting to obtain the suitcase.
The name on the card was Mossadek Hossein.

*　　　*　　　*

Some years ago, before personal radios were so readily
available, it was common practice for constables on patrol to
make a point at telephone kiosks.

In the early hours of one morning the only person to be seen
in the town of Windermere was the constable on patrol. He
made his point and within minutes the telephone rang. On
answering it the constable found it to be the night telephonist at
the local exchange. The telephonist said that a couple from
South Wales, travelling in a car, had rung from a kiosk on the
outskirts of the town, lost, asking the directions to a certain
hotel. He had given them directions and knew they would be
passing the constable shortly.

Sure enough, within minutes, a car appeared and the contable
flagged it down. The driver wound down his window and said:
'Yes Officer?' 'You will be the couple who are staying at the . . . .
Hotel. Just down this road for a quarter of a mile and you will
see it on the left.' A look of complete amazement appeared on
the couples face.

'How on earth do you know where we are going?' asked the

driver. 'Well up here we do like to know who is on our patch, particularly at this hour.' With his mouth open the driver closed his window and drove off.

It was the main talking point at the hotel for days.

*        *        *

**Nottingham Crown Court**
Judge: 'Officer, when did you make up your notes?'
Constable: 'I didn't make them up, my lord, they're true!'

*        *        *

The following is a report submitted by a policewoman in a certain shire force and the reply by her divisional commander—only the names have been changed.

Sir,
### Issue of shirts for policewomen
With reference to the above I have to inform you that on Thursday 18th October all the policewomen at this police station were issued with new shirts, ties and gloves from Quartermasters Stores at FHQ.

On receipt of these shirts it was found that all the shirts issued being collar sizes 13 to $14\frac{1}{2}$ and which normally would have been bust sizes 34″ - 38″ were bust sizes 42″ - 46″. On telephoning the Stores Department about this we were informed that they were aware of the wrong bust sizings of the shirts but they could do nothing other than issue these shirts as they are, as they had no other shirts to issue and no other shirts coming into stock.

On trying on this latest issue of shirts I found that although the neck size was correct the saddle of the shirt came six inches down each arm, the sleeve covered not only my arm but hand and fingers also and the shirt itself, which in my case came out as a bust size of 44″ and I am only bust size 38″, could have been wrapped round twice before buttoning. In addition, when tucked inside my skirt the shirt was long enough to act as an underskirt, and looked very untidy about the waist because of the surplus amount of material.

I respectively request that this report be forwarded to the appropriate department in order that the shirts can be exchanged for correctly fitting uniform shirts.

I submit this on behalf of all the policewomen, none of whom are able to wear any of the shirts with which they have been issued on this occasion.

*B. M. Smith, WPc*

**Reply by divisional commander**
There clearly has been an error here for these shirts were not
intended for general issue they were solely intended for issue to
pregnant policewomen. If we have a shortage of staff with the
necessary qualifications then it may be necessary to take the
required steps for staff to qualify so that we may fill the shirts.

Alternative options would seem to be an issue of padded
bras to policewomen and I would suggest an 'H' cup. This will
entail the fitting of a special shelf by workshops in panda cars
upon which the protuberance may be rested while on patrol.

This action will be supplemented by the Catering Officer
arranging for triple portions of chips to policewomen with issue
of cream cakes and chocolates between meals. Care must be
taken to ensure that the policewomen involved do not indulge in
any exercise which might nullify the effects of the operation.

So far as the length of sleeve is concerned this problem will be
easily met by closing off the cuff and then running lines of
stitching approx 3 inches up from the end of the cuff. There will
be four lines of stitches each $\frac{3}{4}''$ apart thus turning the end of the
sleeves into gloves. This will have the advantage of fitting each
policewomen with white gloves immediately she puts on the
shirt and steps will be taken to recall all white gloves issued to
policewomen as they will be no longer required and
considerable economies effected.

In view of the wealth of material around the waist area this
presents us with the kangaroo syndrome and will be used as a
pouch for, pocketbooks, HORTIs, and personal effects.
Handbags will, therefore, no longer be required and should be
withdrawn, thereby effecting further economies. Dirty shirts
will cater for black glove issue.

*J. Brown, Chief Superintendent*

\*        \*        \*

The sergeant had a new class of recruits at the District Police
Training Centre. At the commencement of each lesson the class
marker would stand in the doorway and as the instructor
entered he would report if any members of the class were absent
and for what reason.

On this particular day, Constable Evans, a well built young
officer, sprang to attention as he entered the classroom and
announced that all were present. He turned away from the

instructor who struck him rather a hard blow to the nape of the neck with his open hand. The constable turned immediately with fists clenched and for a brief moment the instructor thought that he was about to retaliate. 'What was that for, sergeant?' was his question. The instructor replied: 'That's just a reminder Evans lad, that for the next 50 minutes we're going to talk about assaults and woundings.'

The constable returned to his seat at the back of the class and the instructor saw him lean forward and speak to the officer at the next desk. 'What's amusing you now Evans?' he asked. 'Nothing, sergeant,' came the stock reply. 'Come on, now, I'm sure that the whole class wants to share your little joke, not just you and Constable Pearson.' Evans replied: 'All I said to him sergeant, was that I hoped I wasn't on the door on Thursday afternoon when you're dealing with unnatural offences!'

*       *       *

At a magistrates' court a police officer was giving evidence of arrest. 'With the consent of the defendant's landlady, I entered the house and went up to his bedroom, knocked on the door and entered the room where the defendant was in bed with his girlfriend. I said to him that I was a police office and had reason to believe that he could help me with my inquiries into a breaking and entering at such and such, and I requested him to accompany me to the police station. That, your workships, is my evidence.'

The magistrate asked the red-headed defendant if he had any questions to ask. The defendant replied: 'It was nothing like that. He came busting into the room and said: "Nah then, Ginger, hop out of it, you're for the high jump again".'

Which would you believe?

*       *       *

## W. R. C. Chapman, magistrate

Court number three in the Court House was a pleasant room lending itself with equal ease to formal and informal occasion. It looked over the fast-flowing, but very murky, River Derwent. Its only disadvantage was that it was prone to becoming very hot and it was not unusual to see the court usher wrestling with the net curtains to get at the catch to open the windows.

This was the room in which most committal proceedings under the Criminal Justice Act 1967, were heard. There the magistrates' duties were minimal since there is no consideration of evidence, and apart from seeing that all the formalities were complied with and committing the defendant to stand trial in a higher court, their only major responsibility is to determine the issue of bail or custody. One spring day three defendants confronted the magistrates, two in the dock and one, a 17-year-old, in the witness box. All the issues seemed straightforward until defence counsel for the 17-year-old stood up and asked for bail for his client. The alleged offences were grave, he said, but all inquiries were over, there was no chance of interference with the course of duty, it was a serious matter to commit a 17-year-old to prison and his client was unlikely to abscond. The magistrates were clearly in doubt about the last point and no-one seemed in the least surprised when the chairman remanded the youth, together with his two older companions, in custody.

And suddenly the youth was no longer there. He had turned and with a splendid leap had disappeared through the window which was immediately behind the witness box in which he had been stationed. The only constable in court was large in every dimension but in the noble tradition of his service he pursued the miscreant without regard for his own comfort and convenience. Unfortunately the window frame was narrow and the net curtains were like tentacles and in no time he became hopelessly and helplessly wedged and entangled. Justice wears an unruffled face. The magistrates attempted to continue with the business of the court. 'What kind of witness orders are you asking for?' inquired the chairman blandly of the prosecution. But it was impossible not to notice him leaning back beneath the splendid warrant of Her Majesty Queen Elizabeth II, Defender of the faith etc, to get a better view of the absconding miscreant breasting the polluted waters of the River Derwent and making landfall with a hefty baulk of timber in one hand and a large piece of glass in the other. And there he sat prepared to defend himself against all-comers. And come they soon did.

'You're not putting me in custody,' he said, jabbing with his nasty piece of glass at the nearest policeman.

'The only thing to do,' said the officer-in-charge, a man with a literary turn of mind and a quick ear for a pun, 'is to shove the blighter in again and bail him out.' And something of that sort eventually happened.

Meanwhile, back in courtroom number three the face of justice continued unruffled, but the chairman, a kindly man, noticed the youth's mother weeping at the back and sought to say a few soothing words. 'Mrs ......, I'm very sorry that all this has happened, but when you next see your son, do tell him that this kind of behaviour doesn't help anyone, least of all himself.'

She put down the handkerchief. 'He'll catch his death of pneumonia,' she said, 'and all because of you!'

\*       \*       \*

**Richard Horobin, BBC Television producer**
When I was a young reporter, I went to a court which was hearing traffic cases and one officer, giving evidence in a driving without due care and attention case, in answer to a question said: '. . . the visibility was as far as the eye could see.'

\*       \*       \*

A ladies toilet in the town had been broken into during the night and a uniformed policewoman attended. She found that one of the coin-operated machines within the toilet had been forced open and the cash and contents had been stolen. She radioed for the assistance of a scenes of crime officer and shortly afterwards he arrived with his equipment to examine the premises and the machine.

As he finished his job and was packing his equipment into his case two or three ladies entered. On seeing the startled expression on their faces of seeing a man in a ladies toilet, the policewoman raised her hand, pointed her finger at the scenes of crime officer and called out for all to hear: 'I will not tell you again about coming into this toilet. I have warned you before, now please leave before I lock you up.' It was a very red-faced, speechless man who quickly picked up his case and made good his escape.

\*       \*       \*

A panda patrol was sent to see an old lady who was complaining that someone had scrawled a four-letter word on her back gate. Having given the matter appropriate attention, the officer called over the radio to say he was resuming patrol, whereupon the communication-aide quipped: 'Did you tell her what it meant Jack?' 'No,' came the reply, 'just corrected the spelling.' It was amusing to see that the control room message pad had subsequently been endorsed: 'Advice given.'

**A court liaison inspector who had a wealth of experience in courts around Staffordshire has supplied the following examples of humour in court**

Stafford Assizes: Council for the defence: 'My Lord, the accused was about to emigrate to Australia but had only reached Shrewsbury.'

Judge: 'He didn't get very far.'

Counsel: 'No, my Lord, but he was going in the right direction.'

Stafford Assizes: Jury in case of conspiracy to rob being sworn in.

Nervous member of the jury: 'I will well and truly try the several issues between our Sovereign Lady the Queen and the *pensioner* at the bar.'

         ★       ★       ★

At 10pm on 31st December the sergeant was on night duty and took over the sub-division. Just after midnight, and a few minutes into the New Year, he was relieving in the sub-divisional front office. The temperature outside was well below zero and there was at least six inches of snow on the pavement. Around 12.30am a young couple came into the front office and it could be seen from the confetti about them that they were a honeymoon couple. They told the sergeant that a constable a few streets away had informed them that if anyone could help them it was 'Donald down at the nick'.

The sergeant asked them what was their trouble and they told him that they had married in Scotland the previous day, had arranged a late evening flight from Edinburgh to London for their honeymoon, and had written to a hotel in Wimbledon booking a room. When they arrived at the hotel they were told they had no accommodation booked. When the booking form was taken from the files it was discovered that their 12.15am intended time of arrival had been crossed out and 12.30pm inserted. The manager apologised and said that he thought that they had got excited and put the wrong time, and he had altered it to 12.30pm. He now had no vacant rooms, and made little effort to find alternative accommodation for the couple. A constable had heard the heated exchange and had entered the hotel. He had advised them to consult 'Donald' at the 'nick', so they had done just that.

Though the sergeant had a list of local residents from whom

he could seek help in cases of emergency, he decided the lateness of the hour made this quite impractical. The sergeant went on to explain that he could perhaps offer a very modest substitute which was both warm and draught free. He mustered his staff around him and told them what he was intending to do. He would clear a waiting room of furniture, break open the reserve stock room and remove two new cell Dunlopillo mattresses, about half a dozen blankets and two pillows. He would offer the couple a wash and brush up and, after a cup of tea, put them in a the room with a 'Do not disturb' sign on the door.

This was put into effect, and due to the laughter the exercise was causing, and a comment by one of the staff that 'No-one will ever believe them', the sergeant decided to create a 'certificate'. With help from the others on duty a suitable 'certificate' was devised, bearing sealing wax, prisoner's property seals, taxicab badges and impressions of anything that could be found. This was duly presented to the honeymoon couple before they retired, with the promise that at around 7.00am they would be disturbed by the early turn relief with a cup of tea. They were asked to quietly return to the hotel the following morning and not to give publicity to what had happened.

The early turn relief played the game and the couple went on their way. The sergeant went on annual leave.

Three days later the sergeant was relaxing in a seaside hotel when over the radio came the whole story. The BBC would have paid for the couple's honeymoon if they could have traced them.

When the sergeant returned from his period on leave he found an instruction to report to his divisional commander immediately. He did so. The commander had a long list of breaches of the discipline code which an administrator at the Headquarters had formulated. It started with 'You failed to report an incident . . .' and ended with 'You had a female remaining on police premises without a matron or a policewoman present.' When the sergeant pleaded that it was a public relations exercise, and the bride did have her bridegroom with her, and in the circumstances the sergeant had used his discretion, it made little impression.

It all finished with the sergeant receiving a verbal caution: 'You will *never* do that again!'

It was a particularly cold night—there were several degrees of frost. A sergeant and a constable were on a mobile crime prevention patrol on the outskirts of the town when they received a radio message directing them to a fire in the centre of the town. It was 5.00am and the streets were deserted. It took only a few minutes at that time of the day to get to the scene of the fire. The premises burning were a social club and it was well ablaze. The police car arrived at the same time as the first fire appliance and a few inquiries revealed that there would be no persons in the premises.

As usual the firemen were very quickly into action; they located fire hydrants and attached their hoses. One of the hydrants was some one hundred yards from the fire and positioned in the centre of a tree-lined road, and the firemen had fixed a stand-pipe to the eight inch main. Minutes passed and the firemen were doing very well to contain the blaze. In the meantime the sergeant had radioed to headquarters and arranged for barriers to be brought to cordon-off the area. By this time a mixture of mist and smoke had made visibility very poor.

An early morning 'bus came from the direction of the town centre on its way to the dormitory area of the town to collect the early workers. As it made its way along the road the constable saw what was about to happen. Too late he ran into the road in a vain attempt to stop the 'bus. It collided with the stand-pipe and water shot many, many feet into the air, freezing instantly as it hit the branches of the tree and forming a skating-rink on the road.

Both the constable and the sergeant slipped to the floor. Before they could recover, to their horror, they saw a small car coming towards the fountain. The inevitable happened; the car went over the jet and was lifted inches into the air. It came down and spluttered on for a few feet and then came to a halt. Slipping and sliding the two policemen made their way to the car and spent several minutes scraping ice from the car to release the driver.

By this time dawn was breaking to reveal a beautiful yet chaotic scene.

\* \* \*

Sometimes training afforded to the junior members of the service does not reach senior members. A pop festival was held in a deserted part of the county. It was very hilly and the roads were poor. Even worse was the weather. The number of people expected to attend the festival demanded that a large police operation should be put underway. The operation was overlorded by the Assistant Chief Constable (Operations) but the divisional commander was in immediate charge.

The festival was due to finish at 12 midnight and by that time the weather was atrocious. The divisional commander was a chief superintendent who had recently transferred from headquarters administration. The communications officer had armed the chief superintendent with his personal radio set, a transmitter with a separate receiver. The chief superintendent decided that he would leave the police control, which was adjacent to the festival compound, and go to the main entrance of the festival, accompanying him was a superintendent from headquarters. They both squelched their way through a sea of mud and made their way to the entrance. Before they arrived they saw that everything was in a state of chaos.

Thousands of fans were milling about; anxious parents were arriving by car to pick-up their charges and everything was at a standstill. The chief superintendent decided he needed more of his men so he lifted his personal radio and called: 'Tango Bravo Three, Tango Bravo Three, message for you, over.' No reply. 'Tango Bravo Three, Tango Bravo Three', message for you, over.' Again no reply. He was getting angry and lifted the radio lips once more. The superintendent touched him on the arm and said to him: 'That's the receiver you are speaking into, and, in any case, *your* call sign is Tango Bravo Three!'

                         *           *           *

A man in the demolition business had a contract to demolish over three hundred houses. In one of the houses he found a diminutive Irishman and his mates living 'rough'. They refused to leave so he called the police. A rather large constable came to the scene and upon his arrival they scattered. The constable managed to catch hold of the small Irishman and, because he wanted to go after the others, he handcuffed him to the door.

Eventually he came back with another man but found that he had not brought his handcuff key with him. He decided to take 'Paddy' off still manacled to the door. The door was of no value but he insisted on issuing a receipt, eventually returning the door minus 'Paddy'.

A constable was in the sub-divisional headquarters at lunch time when a lady came into report that she had not seen her neighbour, a 95-year-old spinster, for about two days and that the milk was still outside the front door. On the instructions of his sergeant he accompanied the lady to the house in question.

The house was one of a row and the type which had a coal cellar. The lady who informed the police indicated the old lady's bedroom at the rear of the house. The constable drew his staff and banged it loudly on the fall-pipe in an attempt to awake the old lady if she happened to be asleep. No response.

The curtains were all drawn so the constable decided that he must get into the house. The doors were locked and the windows secure. He went to the front of the house and tried the cover on the coal cellar, it was insecure. He lifted it off and with difficulty lowered himself down the hole. It was dark down there, and dirty. Eventually he found his way to the door which connected the cellar with the upper parts of the house. It was locked—on the house side.

With some difficulty the constable extricated himself from the coal-cellar and back into the street. By this time a crowd had collected and it was little wonder that there was more than one smile—the constable was liberally covered with coal dust.

What to do? He decided that he must break into the house. He chose a window at the rear of the house and broke it with his staff. He put his arm through and opened the catch. This enabled him to lift the window and climb through—with no little trepidation. He searched the ground floor but could not find the old lady. He looked down the steps to the cellar in case she had fallen there.

He climbed the stairs rather nervously. All the doors on the landing were closed. He opened the first—it was a box-room; he opened the second, it was bare. The third door had to be opened. As he did so, slowly, the constable sensed that this was the room. He stepped into the room and, behind the door, he saw a double bed and in the centre of that bed a dear old lady—wide awake and very indignant.

'Are you all right, madam?' asked the constable.

'Of course I am young man,' replied the lady. 'What are you doing in here, is there no privacy in a person's own home?'

'But, but, we thought . . .'

'You have no right to break into houses and frighten

respectable people. If I want to stay in bed all day why shouldn't
I? I'll speak to your superiors tomorrow about this. It's not
decent. What will people say . . .'

The constable backed out of the room and beat a hasty
retreat. Once outside he took a deep breath, calmed himself and
assured the lady who had visited the police station that
everything was in order.

This lady could see his embarrassment and apologised most
profusely. There remained the matter of the broken window but
the lady assured the officer that her brother would fix that.

Relieved, the constable went on his way.

*          *          *

Murphy's second law applies to panda cars—this law
paraphrased says that if it is at all possible for a panda car to be
damaged, it will be. Foxes run from hedgerows and smash fog
lamps; grouse fly off the moors and shatter windscreens; cows
walking down country lanes lean on cars and dent panels.
Things happen to panda cars which never happen to private
cars. Here is one perfectly true example.

A constable had to check a secondary school and instead of
leaving the car in the road outside and walking in, he drove into
the playground. (A future generation of police officers will
surely be born without feet!)

It was dark but his headlights didn't pick out a metal netball
post until the very last moment, he swerved and missed the post
but in doing so, he ran over the metal base-plate. The effect of
this was to bring the post crashing down on to the roof of the car
creating a very neat diagonal 'crease'.

*          *          *

Scene: Woman calls into inquiry office of police station at
noon.
Constable: 'Yes, madam, can I help you?'
Woman: 'I want to report the theft of my telly.'
Constable: 'When did this happen?'
Woman: 'About this time yesterday.'
Constable: 'How do you know?'
Woman: 'Well, you see. I had been to the corner shop and when I
was coming back I approached my house from the side and I
saw a man carrying it out to a van at the front, and then drive
off.'
Constable: 'Why didn't you tell us immediately?'

Woman (wagging her finger in the constable's face): 'Oh I know your type and the naughty tricks you get up to, so I thought I would give him a fair chance . . . !'
(Eventually the thief was caught after doing several other 'jobs')

*       *       *

Scene: Woman meets constable in street and reports theft of purse. Three weeks pass and woman meets same constable in the street.
Woman: 'Have you recovered my purse yet?'
Constable: 'Sorry my dear, no, and it is unlikely we will.'
Woman: 'I can't understand it, if it had been Dixon of Dock Green he would have cleared it all up in half an hour!'

*       *       *

The station sergeant had had a very arduous and trying day—the 'phone had been ringing incessantly and there had been a constant trail of visitors to the station. The 'phone rang again, the caller had lost her canary. To which the weary sergeant replied as politely as possible: 'Very well, madam, I shall turn out the Flying Squad immediately.'

*       *       *

**The first panda patrol?**
Bath-chairs were commonplace at one time and about 2am one summer's morning, an alert constable spotted one and to prevent it from being stolen decided to take it to the police station. En route, the main road, dimly lit and thankfully deserted, sloped gently downhill making his task much easier; but why walk when one could ride? With an extra push he sprang aboard and sat down with face beaming and cape flying in the breeze. The wheels bumped over the stones as the chair gathered speed and hurtled on at an alarming rate.

The grin on the constable's face changed to one of grim determination as he struggled unsuccessfully to control the wretched, brakeless flying machine.

He did his best with a means of locomotion built for a more leisurely existence but the outcome was inevitable . . . Bang! the cursed thing tipped over on striking the kerb and became a tangled mess with a dazed constable amongst the wreckage, peering into the stern face of an irate night-duty inspector, who had appeared from nowhere.

Traffic in London is now controlled by computer and it works fairly well.

On one occasion several years ago it was a difficult job for police on the old London Bridge to get traffic moving on the north and south lanes.

A frustrated Met chief inspector walked across the bridge to the hard pressed City police and said: 'For goodness sake give the northbound a run quick, mate; we've just had a message from the Brighton Police that the tide's coming in over the last vehicle in the tailback!'

*          *          *

True story told to Rev G.J. F. Langan, Wimbledon, by a prison officer: The prison officer was in the dock with the accused. The forewoman of the jury returned with the jury and asked the judge: 'If we find the prisoner guilty how much will you give him?' Apparently the judge nearly had a stroke.

*          *          *

A lady had been accused of gambling at the time when it was an offence. The club in which she played cards had been raided again and she came up before the stipendiary magistrate at Marylebone. She was fined £150. Her English was not good and she asked the magistrate: 'Please, sir, can I pay the fine slowly?' Magistrate: 'Yes, slowly—on your way out!'

*          *          *

A police officer on leave was driving a very old Ford car to Scotland some years ago. He saw that he was approaching a junction controlled by a constable. He switched the indicator to show he wanted to turn but, due to some mechanical malfunction both of the semaphore signals came out simultaneously.

The constable on traffic control walked slowly over to the driver's window: 'Tell me, sir, are you about to turn left, right or are you using this road as a b..... runway?'

*          *          *

Workers in any profession will agree, I am sure, that the early turn is difficult. It is difficult to arise, difficult to be bothered about eating at that time of day, difficult even, particularly in the midst of winter, to get dressed correctly. Nevertheless a police officer is expected to be smart when he reports for duty. One cold January morning the inspector paraded the relief at

6.00am. 'Brummy', the inspector, a native of Birmingham, was a good officer, well liked by everyone; but he did have his off moments—particularly when he was suffering from his personal problem, gout.

This morning he had a very painful attack; he'd had very little sleep, consequently he was far from being in the best of moods. After the men on parade had produced their staff, handcuffs and whistles he hobbled around to inspect the three ranks.

Fortunately he did not see the concealed smiles. He was interested in other things. The boots which were not up to standard, trousers which needed a touch of the iron, the creased collar. He had something to say to most of the men that morning.

As he returned to his lectern from which he would impart information prior to sending the men to their respective beats, a voice came from the centre rank: 'Permission to speak sir.' Rather taken aback the inspector gave his permission.

'I thought you ought to know, sir, that you are wearing a red tie this morning.'

Sure enough he was; in his rush and in his pain that morning, instead of tying on his regulation black tie, he had picked-up a brilliant crimson creation. But it was no more crimson than his face.

*         *         *

A part of one of the Command Courses held at the Police College concentrates on interviewing techniques. A lecture is given by an acknowledged expert in this field and then time is set aside for practical application.

One thing is emphasised, that personal bias should never intervene into the process, but it is accepted that this facet is very difficult to eradicate.

On one occasion, for the practical session, the scenario provided was as follows: There is a vacancy for a chief inspector, deputy sub-divisional commander in a county force. Applications have been received from five inspectors. The panel is to interview each applicant to find the most suitable. Realism is essential and, for realism, the 'candidates' have been chosen from inspectors who are at the College on a course. The members of the Command Course are divided into panels; on one panel are two superintendents, a male and a female chief inspector. Each candidate is shown in and interviewed at depth by each member of the panel in turn. The third candidate was very very smart but had a grim countenance. The interview went ahead and it came the turn of the woman chief inspector. She asked a few preliminary questions and then asked: 'What role do you see for a woman in the police service?' The inspector thought for a few moments and then replied: 'I must be frank. I think that too much emphasis is placed on the value of women in the police service. I realise there is a need for women for a few specialist tasks, but it is my opinion that this could be done, in the main, by matrons. I cannot see the need for full-time policewomen.'

It was obvious that this was not play acting; he really meant what he was saying. It was also obvious that the woman chief inspector did not like it. Her subsequent questions were distinctly hostile but the inspector did not change his stance. The chairman of the panel sensed the atmosphere and concluded the interview.

The final candidate was interviewed and then it is was time for the panel to decide who was the most suitable applicant. They discussed all the applicants and the male members of the panel were unanimous in their decision that the third applicant was the best. His experience was far better than the rest and in other respects he was the most acceptable. It was not unanimous though, the woman chief inspector said that in her estimation he was totally unsuitable for the advertised vacancy. The chairman asked: 'Why?'

'Because he's ugly!' was the reply.

So much for objective interviewing!

*        *        *

At the Police Staff College mess evenings are held regularly and, of course, are very, very formal. On these evenings the opportunity is taken of inviting distinguished guests from all walks of life. Though the domestic arrangements are the responsibility of the staff, a great deal of responsibility lies with whoever may be, for the time being, the Mess President supported by his Vice-President.

There is a certain form to be followed and the President and his 'Vice' are tutored by the staff officer. Amongst many other things they are told that when the meal finishes and the port has circulated, the President rises, strikes his gavel twice, and calls upon the Vice-President in these terms: 'Mr Vice, The Queen!'

In response the Vice-President proposes the Loyal Toast. It must be mentioned here that the dining hall at the college is very long and while the President sits on the 'top table', Mr Vice sits at a table at the far end.

For one mess evening the President was a superintendent from a Midlands force, his Vice was a chief inspector from a neighbouring force who had a distinctive Birmingham accent—he also had a keen, yet, sometimes strange sense of humour. When the evening was being discussed with the staff officer the need for propriety was mentioned and the chief inspector said that in response to 'Mr Vice, The Queen', he would reply (because of the distance involved): 'Yer what'. That would have been a catastrophe.

The evening came and the President and his Vice greeted the guests in the bar and when they were all gathered they processed to the dining hall where all the other students together with their guests were assembled. As they walked over the President could not dispel from his mind that the very formal evening would degenerate into a farce if the chief inspector did, in fact, reply as he had suggested he would. And this on the night that the Home Secretary was the principal guest!!!

The meal was finished, the port had been passed around and the time had arrived for the President to call upon the Vice-President. Slowly he rose, hoping against hope that the unpredictable chief inspector would behave with due decorum. He brought the gavel down, not on the block of wood, but on the bowl of a desert spoon which went into orbit somewhere in the distance, much to the amusement of the assembly, but to the total despair of the President. In the distance the President heard his Vice intone, in a perfectly modulated voice, 'Her Majesty, The Queen'.

*    *    *

At a local show a little girl had become separated from her parents and was crying bitterly. She was taken to the police tent where a kindly policewoman tried in vain to get the little girl to give her name.

In desperation, she looked at the back of the girl's coat to see if she had her name on it. But no!

Then in a flash of inspiration the policewoman said: ' I know who are you, you are Polyester.' 'I'm not, I'm not,' said the girl through her tears, 'I'm Sarah' and then gave her name.

A policeman's organisation in Georgia ran a contest for 'the best excuse for speeding.' One driver said that he was speeding to a service station before his brakes failed. Another said that his wife was working at a summer camp for 20 kids that stuttered, as a cook. That night they had had a farewell party for her and by the time the kids had expressed their appreciation he had to hurry to make up for lost time.

*       *       *

An indent to Police Headquarters stores for uniform for members of the Special Constabulary contained the following item:

'Eight pairs of Special Constabulary flashers . . .'

*       *       *

A report from a constable on a rural beat panda car, submitted on 30th March, stated that damage had been caused to the front of his car by a hare which had run into it from the hedgerow. The divisional commander submitted it to vehicle records at headquarters with the following comment: 'The local hares are mad at this time of the year'. An inspector pencilled in a marginal note: 'I bet this one was particularly incensed at what happened to him!'

*       *       *

During a very staid lecture on 'leadership' at a training college the speaker was expounding on the natural leaders which emerge in situations, not only within the human race but also in the world of wildlife.

'Imagine,' he said 'a flock of birds migrating in the autumn. They form a 'V' shape with one bird at the apex. That one bird has emerged as a leader of the group.'

'He's no leader,' quipped a voice from the back. 'He's the only one who knows the B..... way!'

*       *       *

After an accident a constable had difficulty in convincing his sergeant that he knew what he was talking about.

'PC Martin here, sarge. I've reported that accident.'

'Everything all right then?'

'Yes, Ryder's gone to hospital.'

'Got it now. What about the driver?'

'He was a Walker.'

'Are you quite sober, Martin? I'm asking about the driver.'
'That's right, sarge, it was a bus by the way, the driver was Walker.'
'What have you done with the bike?'
'What bike?'
'If he was a rider, Martin, he must have a bike.'
'That's his name, sarge, Ryder. He was walking.'
'Now, Martin, let's get this straight. The driver was walking?'
'No sarge, his name was Walker.'
'I see. Better let the inspector know about this one. Sir, got an accident here. A Ryder knocked down by a Walker. No, I'm not drunk, sir. Let me explain . . .'

\*　　　\*　　　\*

### Lord Ted Willis

The following story illustrates the contrast between the British Police and the American.

In New York a man who was stopped for speeding was approached by an irate copper armed with a huge revolver in his holster who pulled him out of the car and said: 'Hey leadfoot, where's the fire?'

By contrast a motorist was driving up the Mall one day just as the Horseguards were riding by. As he got near them his entire exhaust and silencer system fell off and rolled under the first horseman. The horse reared and threw the guardsman, upsetting the rest of the troop.

Meanwhile the motorist swerved causing a motor cyclist to crash and the motor car itself finished half-way up a tree. A British policeman strolled over to him, looked in the window and said: 'We *are* having trouble today, aren't we, sir?'

\*　　　\*　　　\*

This story concerns a constable who was a well-known character. He was a big, big man and had the face of a boxer and, indeed had been a very good boxer. He was afraid of no man.

One Monday morning after a drunk had been found guilty by the stipendiary magistrate, after having pleaded not guilty, the magistrate called the boxer constable to the witness box. 'Tell me, officer, since I have been on this bench, every Monday morning you have had before me a drunk and disorderly or a drunk and incapable, tell me how do you differentiate between the two?' After a moment's thought the constable replied:

'It's like this your worship. On Saturday nights they send me down to Chelsea Street and when the pubs turn-out I stands by a pub door, and as they come out I stick my foot out. Them as falls over it and stays down are drunk and incapable and them as gets up and wants to fight are drunk and disorderly.'

*       *       *

The scene was a Scottish motorway on a dark and icy evening; a motorcyclist stands beside a stationary Honda.

Enter two traffic patrol officers. 'What's the trouble?' 'I've run out of petrol.' The gallant officers volunteer to collect and bring it back to the unfortunate traveller.

They return with a tinful of two star. But what's this. The petrol cap is frozen on. The motorcyclist suggests a lighted match to unfreeze it but the traffic patrol point out the possible consequences. 'Why not,' asks one of the worthy constables, 'Why not try the old fashioned remedy.' The motorcyclist expresses some embarassment but the second constable is getting cold and impatient so he performs the deed quickly and efficiently. Both the car and the motorcycle roar off into the dark.

About a fortnight later the chief constable receives a letter thanking him for the help and courtesy given by his officers to the writer's daughter.

*       *       *

A selection of genuine howlers from Criminal Record Office records published in the Essex Police magazine:
'Dentures upper jaw, bottom in poor condition.'
'Appendix scar on right thigh.'
'Left testicle removed, small scar centre of forehead.'
'Sometimes wears no hat.'

*       *       *

Often enthusiasm can lead to a loss of dignity. A first division soccer match was being played and some 40 policemen reported for duty at the ground. They were briefed by a superintendent who told them, amongst many other things, to deal with incidents calmly, with tact and create a good impression on the large crowd which was expected. One of the constables was a keen man, a very enthusiastic officer. He was quite a young man but had a tendency to be impetuous. He had a very pleasant nature and was well liked and trusted by his colleagues and superiors alike.

He was detailed to patrol the touchline close to the boys' 'pen'. The ground filled up quickly and it was obvious that there would be a capacity crowd. By 2.45pm this proved to be the case. The boys' enclosure was particularly full. This enclosure was at pitch level in one corner of the ground.

The constable was walking backwards and forwards over a distance of some 15 yards. The match was underway and after about 15 minutes there was a stoppage. The boys in their enclosure were packed liked sardines and one had had enough. He was about 12 years old and he scrambled over the wall on to the path surrounding the pitch. The constable told him to get back. Instead of responding the lad ducked under the constable's outstretched arm and ran off diagonally across the pitch towards the popular side in the opposite corner.

It was not important, play was not, at that moment, taking place, but the constable's impetuosity took over—he set off in hot pursuit. The lad had a very good start but by the time he reached the half-way line there was only about ten yards between them. By this time the crowd of some 35,000 was cheering (it can be safely said the boy, not the constable).

The constable stumbled—an even greater cheer. He was determined, he carried on and again began to gain ground on the lad.

He almost caught up with the boy when they ran out of pitch. The boy dived over the fence surrounding the pitch into the crowd to be caught by spectators.

The constable managed to decelerate and came to rest at the fence, but his helmet carried on, into the crowd—never to be seen again.

The superintendent spoke to the constable after the game!

*       *       *

It was half-way through the afternoon relief and at the sub-divisional headquarters some officers were having their refreshment period. The station sergeant came into the canteen and said that a suicide had been reported a few streets away and detailed two constables to leave their meal and make their way immediately to the house where the tragedy had taken place.

One constable had several years service behind him but the other was rather a raw probationer. As they left the station they checked the time and found it to be 5.45pm. Within a few minutes they were at the scene; to be followed quickly by an ambulance.

The kitchen door was open and inside the body of a middle-aged woman lay on the floor, her head still in the oven. The senior constable assisted the two ambulancemen in their unpleasant task while the probationer looked-on, pale faced, trying to compose himself—it was his first sudden death! Also at the scene was the next door neighbour—a man of advanced years but still active and particularly talkative. When the ambulancemen had left the senior constable said that he would examine the scene and attempt to find the woman's husband and other witnesses. The old chap had already offered the information, many times, that it was he who had found the body.

The probationer was deputed to take his statement. Together they went to the man's house and into his parlour. The young constable took out his pocket book and pen. While he was doing this the old man was bent over the sideboard; when he straightened up he had two glasses and two pint-sized bottles of 'dinner ale'.

'Here you are lad, get this down you.' said the man, passing over a large glass and one of the bottles.

'No thanks,' replied the constable, 'I don't drink much. Anyway I was half-way through my tea when we were sent around here.'

'Look lad. I buy five of these bottles every night of my life. If anyone comes to see me they share them with me. Come on, down with it!' It was obvious that if the constable did not do as he was told, he would get no statement, so he accepted.

It was hard work taking the statement. Though the old man was willing to make a statement, he also had a captive audience to hear his life story. The time passed and as it did so the young constable drank his beer with constant prompting from the old man. He was pleased when the bottle was empty—but his pleasure was short-lived; he was presented with a second bottle. He tried to refuse but to no avail.

Slowly he extracted more of the statement and painfully continued to partake of the refreshment. He had finished the statement and nearly finished the beer when there was a knock on the door. The old man opened it and there, standing on the step, was the sub-divisional inspector. He came into the room. 'Have you finished lad? You could have taken 20 statements by now!' he announced. He then espied the beer bottles and glasses—and the constable's red face.

'Would you like a drink as well?' asked the old man, 'Your mate seems to like it.'

'No thank you,' the inspector's reply was decidedly chilly. 'Let's have you Jones, back to the station!'

Back at the station the inspector threatened to 'throw the book' at Jones, whose protestations fell on deaf ears. It was a long time before he was allowed to forget his drinking session.

*       *       *

New garage accommodation was being built at divisional headquarters and during the course of construction temporary accommodation was found in some local authority buildings about one mile from headquarters. One morning, before the lunch break a mechanic was working on the engine of patrol car NA 404 and by the time he ceased work for the morning he had completed a good deal of the work on the engine. The car was in the open parked in a yard where it was usual to park patrol cars when not in use. He left the bonnet open and went for his lunch. During the lunch break the traffic inspector called into the temporary garage just as it started to rain. He saw the open bonnet of the car and the engine exposed to the elements and with much muttering about the quality of present day mechanics he closed it and, as a second thought, removed the key from the ignition, took it into the sergeant's office and hung it on the keyboard. Shortly after he left.

About 1.50pm the early turn began to arrive at the garage to park their cars ready for them to be taken over by the afternoon shift which would parade at 2.00pm.

At 2.00pm the sergeant paraded his shift in the office. The telephone rang as he was about to detail the men to their respective cars and areas. He picked up the telephone and a brief conversation ensued. When he had finished he said: 'Jones and Smith you are on area 'B'. There's an abnormal load on the ring-road on its way north, pick it up and get rid of it as soon as possible—nip out there straight away. He looked at the keyboard and said take 404.' The constables did as they were bid and instilled with the urgency of disposing quickly of the abnormal load they omitted the usual checks which were always undertaken before taking a car over and commencing patrol.

The driver climbed into his seat, the engine fired first time and they were on their way. The ring-road was only two miles distant and the load was soon picked up. After a brief exchange with the crew of the load they started the escort.

The mechanic returned from his lunch fortified and ready for an afternoon of hard graft. He looked into the yard and inquired where 404 was.

'Out on patrol,' replied the sergeant.

In less time than it takes to tell the situation and its gravity 'sank-in'. The sergeant was left with the dilemma of how he should get in touch with the crew of 404 without disclosing too much over the radio. With a brief explanation to the reserve driver and an instruction to him to get astride a motor cycle and 'find those two in 404 and stop them before the engine blows up' the sergeant grabbed for the microphone.

'Hallo 404—check your engine!'

'Repeat, please,' came the polite reply.

'Stop your car and check the engine.' The urgency in the sergeant's voice brought the car to a halt and the abnormal load pulled in close behind.

'See,' said the driver, 'he saw us drive out without checking the car and he's trying to be funny.'

Just at that moment the police motorcyclist arrived at a fast rate of knots, stopped his machine and strolled back to the two constables who, by that time, had lifted the bonnet and were looking into the engine compartment. The driver of the load joined them and looked in. The driver of the police car later said that he was intrigued by the void where the radiator should have been but he could not understand at the time what should have been there—he went cold all over when he did realise the radiator was missing.

The driver of the abnormal load spoke: 'You've got no radiator,' he said, scratching his head.

'No,' replied the police driver, 'this is one of those new, modified versions, it's air-cooled.'

The truth dawned and everyone laughed, but this laughter was short-lived. The sergeant and a constable arrived with a relief car.

404 was towed back to the temporary garage and the repair

work was completed. No permanent damage was caused to the car by its outing and it proved to be one of the best cars in the fleet until it was eventually retired. The episode was a very close-kept secret!

\*         \*         \*

It was the custom if a serving member or a police pensioner died, for a burial party to attend from the local division. This normally comprised an inspector and six constables.

Notification was received that a pensioner who had retired some 20 years before had died and that the funeral was to be held at 2.00pm the following Friday; the cortege to leave the home of the widow.

At 1.30pm on the day, an inspector arrived together with the six constables. The inspector went to announce their arrival while the constables waited outside. Within a few seconds a man came out and introduced himself as the pensioner's son. He invited them into the house for a drink. None was particularly interested at that time of the day but did not think it proper, in the circumstances, to refuse. Except one, George. He was an oft professed tee-totaler. He refused politely, explaining his aversion to alcohol. The other five went in to be handed a half-pint glass of mild beer. There were about a dozen or so mourners including the widow; all appeared to be drinking beer.

A few minutes later the door opened and in walked George. The son asked him if he was sure he wouldn't have a glass of beer. After a pause George replied: 'Well all right then.' To the utter amazement of all his colleagues. The son indicated that perhaps he would help himself from the sideboard. George went over to the sideboard on which there were several bottles and uncorked a bottle of port, almost filled the tumbler and knocked it back. Everyone was watching him, everything was quiet. One of his fellow constables broke the silence.

'Hey, George, I thought you were tee-total!'

'Oh, yes,' George replied, 'but I'm only beer tee-total!'

\*         \*         \*

Every Saturday evening the Irish element in a part of a Midlands town arranged a dance for themselves in a local dance hall. It was a simple affair with some two hundred people attending the rather dilapidated venue. No intoxicating liquor was on sale (officially). The only refreshment available was obtained at a makeshift snack-bar where the customers could buy tea, coffee, soft drinks, biscuits, crisps and ice-cream.

This did not mean that it was like a Band of Hope meeting— often far from it. Though the dance commenced at 8.00pm, the majority did not arrive until after closing time, usually the worse for drink. There was not a lot of trouble but the sergeant always arranged to have a constable outside when the dance finished.

Normally the customers would loiter around outside for 15 or 20 minutes then would wander or stagger to their homes. After they had disappeared, the constable would usually go back into the shabby dance hall and be treated to a cup of tea and maybe a biscuit before the organisers locked-up.

When he paraded for duty at 10.00pm, Sergeant Black posted Constable Williams to area 23 and reminded him to be outside the 'Scala' dance hall at closing time.

Ten minutes before the appointed time Williams arrived outside the dance hall and could very clearly hear the revellers inside. After five minutes the sergeant arrived. They stood talking and shortly the first departing dancers appeared. Gradually they were joined by others until there was a large crowd outside. Very noisy but all good-humoured—obviously they were in no hurry to go their respective ways.

A shout came from within the hall and the sergeant and constable went in. They saw two men rolling on the floor more playing than fighting. Constable Williams parted them, lifted them to their feet and directed them through the door and on their way. Both went peacefully showering the constable with blessings as they left, now reconciled one with the other. Williams looked around him. The sergeant was standing in the snack-bar talking to an organiser, so Williams went to join them. Both he and the sergeant were wearing greatcoats.

When he got to the bar the organiser asked if they would care for a drink; the sergeant had tea, the constable coffee. They were asked if they would have something to eat and the sergeant replied that he would like a biscuit. Looking on the constable saw the sergeant receive two packages which he promptly put into the depths of his pocket. Williams had to be satisfied with his coffee. They had almost finished their drinks when there was shouting outside. Out they went to find the two men fighting again in the road. This time the sergeant separated them but it took some ten minutes to persuade them to move along. Eventually they went, this time blessing the sergeant.

It was another 15 minutes before all the dancers had gone their various ways.

When the last had disappeared the sergeant said to Williams: 'Make an entry in your book, I'll sign it later. Oh, yes, you'd better have one of these biscuits.' He plunged his hand into his pocket. It remained there and a look of dismay crossed his face. Slowly he drew his hand from the pocket. It was wet, it was sticky; the 'biscuits' were, or had been, choc-ices!

*       *       *

The following is part of a report submitted by a policewoman, the secretary of the force netball section, to the superintendent, secretary of the central sports committee asking for a request to be circulated to the force inviting interested members to join the section.

Superintendent Jones,
   Sir,
       With reference to the above section. Over the past four years the section has been successful in winning numerous trophies within this area. However, *due to circumstances beyond anyone's control* some of the section have now become pregnant and are leaving the section . . . it is now hoped that we can fill these positions with other, experienced, policewomen.

*       *       *

The following is a contribution from an inspector in Surrey:

As a raw constable I was posted to a division on the other side of the county. I had never heard of the place, let alone been there, and as you can imagine I had to quickly learn my bearings.

Having already toured my new beat on my bicycle on one of the 'settling in' days before reporting to my new station, I was certain I would need a map and so obtained one.

Even though I had such a short length of service, because I was from another division and not on a 'first time posting' I was treated by my colleagues as an old man almost from day one. All except for my sergeant! We made points in those days, and he was one of those sergeants who believed that supervision consisted solely of catching his men out. Needless to say, it kept every constable, including myself, on his toes. But is also gave me my first training in how to be crafty, a much needed asset in this job!

During my first few days at the new station this particular sergeant arrived at almost every point I made, usually just as the last minute expired, and, of course, I would be there for exactly five minutes. He particularly made sure to meet me at my points before and after a meal break. 'Book me 5', he would call as he passed in the 'Supervisory Vehicle' (one of only two cars at the station). From the tales told to me by fellow constables, I was aware that if ever I was absent from a point (no personal radios!) he would be certain to visit it and his wrath would know no bounds.

So it transpired that, after about a week, I was given an outlying beat with hourly points, which took me at least three miles from my home. I made all the points and arrived, breathless, at each one. I had one more point to make and that was near my home—the point before my meal break. Strangely enough I had not seen the sergeant once that morning and I had an uneasy feeling that I had gone to the wrong points. I checked my beat book, but no—the points were shown were the ones I had made. I had marked them all on my trusty map!! As I was then leaving the penultimate point I looked at my map and figured out a way to cut across country, through a private estate which was part of my patrol area although I had not previously travelled the route.

I pedalled for what seemed to be at least four miles, and, as the time was drawing near to the next point, panic set in when I realised that I was totally lost and disorientated. I had cycled off the map!

I eventually reached a signpost which showed my destination as being $3\frac{1}{2}$ miles away, and I had about 15 minutes until the deadline of my pre-meal break point.

With thoughts of discipline offences, with me still a probationer, and an irate sergeant, plus a burnt-out dinner waiting for me I can still remember the sweat which dripped from my forehead—partly from the strenuous pedalling but mostly from fear!

The saying 'necessity is the mother of invention' certainly rang true for me that day, and when a builder's van approached the junction where I stood painfully scrutinising my map, I decided that immediate action was required. The van pulled to a halt at my signal and I approached the driver. We looked at each other for a second or two and then we recognised each other. An old friend I had not seen for several years! I rapidly explained the situation and within seconds my bike was in the back of his van and we were hot-foot to my point. Relief turned to roars of laughter when we neared the fateful telephone kiosk. I had at least three minutes to spare and coming in the other direction was the sergeant in the police car. We drove on past the point to the next bend in the road. I hopped out and thanked my friend for his life-saving kindness and made a mental note to repay the favour some day.

I then cycled towards my point, from the direction I should have been travelling had I not got lost and arrived, fully recovered and not in the least out of breath, although, perhaps, still showing signs of the previous fatigue.

My sergeant could not understand why he had not passed me on the way to the point, and I just smiled and let him wonder. He guessed I had been up to something, but would never know for sure.

I still had one laugh to come because, after waiting the full five minutes with him (he knowing that I would then have to cycle hard again to get to my home for lunch and then back to the same point afterwards) when he tried to start the car it just did not want to know. It spluttered and sounded as if the carburettor had flooded. We both knew that the mechanic would be at his lunch and so a long wait was in store for the sergeant.

I left him thumping the phone box in anger at getting, apparently, very little assistance from the station officer who was no doubt chuckling even more than I.

*

Perhaps the old saying should apply: 'Non illegitamus carborundum'—(don't let the b...... wear you down!)

*          *          *

# CARTOONS

FA CUP
DRAW

CHELSEA v TOTTENHAM
WEST BA v COVENTRY
LONCASTR v CHELSEA
QPR v CRYSTAL P
or OPT...

*Chelsea are at home to Spurs. Your next of kin
have already been notified !*

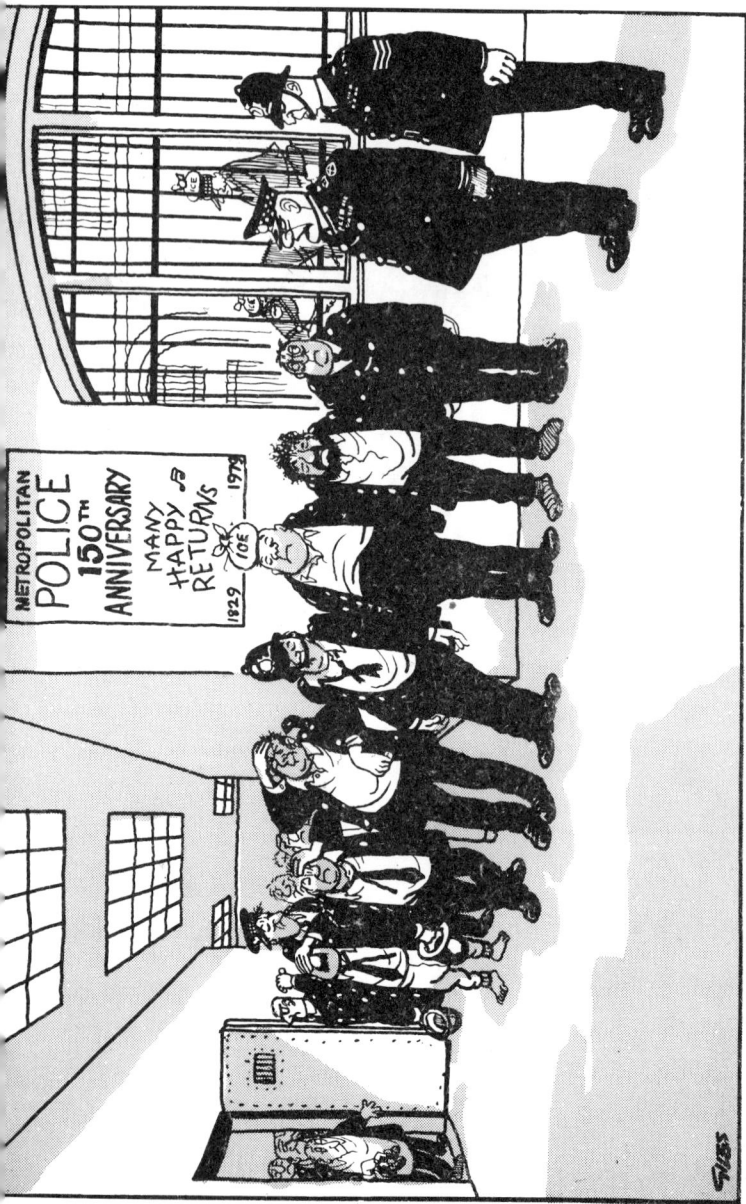

"Great for our public image — the nick bunged full of drunk and disorderly birthday revellers"

"Goody, goody, our getaway car—what kept yer Percy?"

"It's not often I see eye to eye with chief constables"

THEY SAY CAN WE SPARE A COPPER, SIR —
FOR THEIR BONFIRE!

"That one will go far—booked the Chief Constable for lingering with intent outside police HQ"

"May my first case of the day be a rail striker—six years minimum!"

"I want you all to go out there and restore our image — and you, Wilson, keep your hat on at all times"

"We demand police protection from independent bodies taking pictures of us at work"

"Do you ever wonder who wrote their scripts?"

"Yes, there are a lot of little comforts I shall miss when we go back to the Scrubs"

"What comments did you let Grandma add on the bottom of that census form?"

"Don't go away son—me and my mate are just going to have a consultation whether we thump your head or kick your backside"

"Smuggling booze into the game in an empty after-shave lotion bottle wasn't very canny, Angus"

"One small modification of the rules—no one goes over the wall to get their ball back."

HM PRISONS
FREE GOLF
LESSONS FOR
PRISONERS.

NEW BALLS

"Look, sonny—we've had enough hoax bear stories for one year—so get your stuffed gorilla out of here"

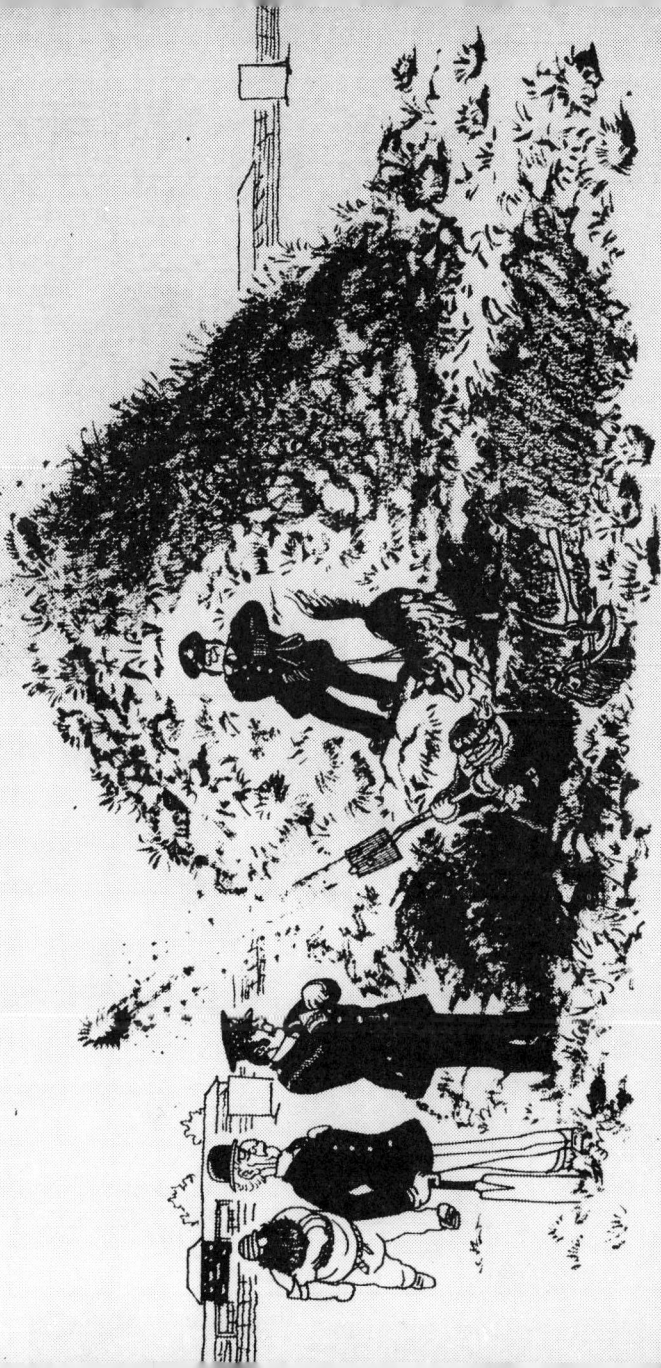

"We appreciate your enthusiastic protest against apartheid Lady, but the Barbarians are not playing rugby at Lords"

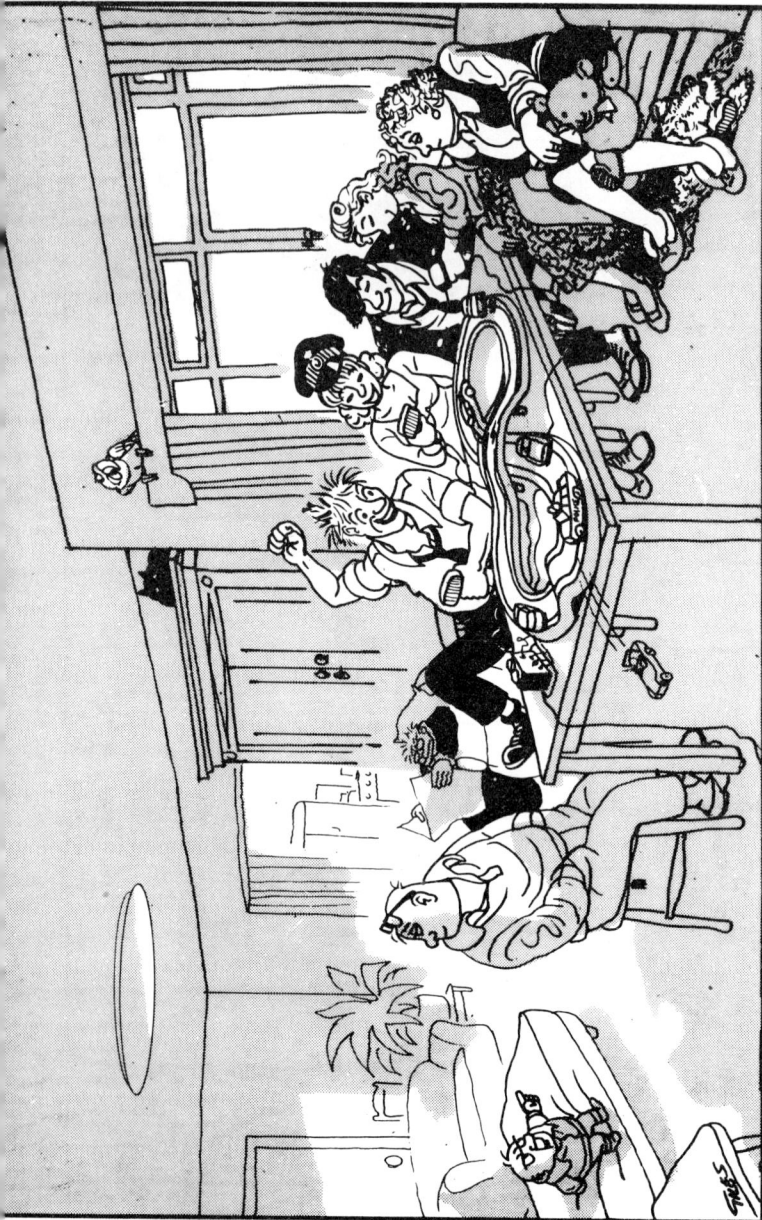

"Giving the Police extra powers doesn't entitle their new copper boyfriends to monopolise my electric Highway Patrol!"

"The line on the floor tests drunks and if anybody walks up the wall we know they're on drugs"

"Hello Control . . . I've located that hijacked beer lorry . . . "

"I've been assigned to a Nudist Camp for a month . . ."

# HUMOROUS MISCELLANY

In my collection I have many stories, jokes and miscellaneous examples of humour which do not easily fit into separate categories therefore I have brought these together in the following section. The intention of bringing together humorous tales, jokes and anecdotes in a book had been in my mind for several years. At the same time I was conscious of the need of various national police charities to raise funds. The idea slowly dawned that if I could catalogue my material and publish the result, I could satisfy my desire and, at the same time, benefit the charities.

To make the task worthwhile, I decided that I should solicit material from other members of the service so I wrote to the editor of the weekly police journal, the *Police Review*. A couple of weeks passed before the letter was published.

On the whole the media has been kind to the service, there have been notable exceptions, but generally speaking, coverage has been fair. However, there must have been a 'blind-spot'. Events which followed the publication of that letter in the *Police Review* demonstrated that newspaper, radio and television editors had never thought that there could be anything remotely funny about, or within, the police service. The *Police Review* arrives with the subscriber on Friday and I thought that a few days, or perhaps a few weeks, would pass before there was any response. I was wrong. The first reaction came shortly after 6pm on the day it was published.

I had just cleared my desk and was walking towards the door when my telephone rang. I put down my brief case and lifted the the receiver. Fully expecting to have a last minute query from a colleague, I announced myself. The voice I heard had a North American accent; it was a female voice. 'Is that Superintendent Harris?'

'Yes, can I help you?' I replied.

'This is a presenter on CBC radio news, Canada, speaking. We go live in two minutes and would like to interview you concerning your new book will you help?'

It took some seconds to recapture some of my composure. We then had a discussion for some five minutes. The contents of that discussion I could not remember the moment the interview ended, much less now. What I did not realise at that time was that was only the beginning. On the Saturday morning I had a call from a reporter on a national Sunday newspaper. That was all that day and the next. On Monday things really 'took-off'. For the next ten days it was apparent that not only police officers read the *Police Review*. I lost count of the number of reporters, newspapers, both national and local, who wanted an interview. What surprised me even more was the number of radio and television stations whose imaginations were captured. During the next few days I was interviewed, either live or recorded, on seven local radio stations, Radio One, Radio Two, Radio Four, BBC television and Associated television.

I had only sought publicity and contributions from within the police service but had received publicity nationwide. The contributions began to flow in and over a period of several months I received several thousand. I was grateful, and deeply moved, that so many people should show so much interest. It showed me, too, that there is a wealth of humour concerning the police service and that the members of the police service were not the only source.

I had been interviewed on radio before, but the events of those few days will stay in my mind for ever. Several interviews provided their own moments of humour which are worth relating.

One morning, about 10am, I answered my telephone. At the other end was an ATV producer. He asked me if I would be willing to record an interview with one of his reporters for transmission that evening. I agreed and asked when I would be wanted. He replied that the reporter and crew were *already on the way* and would arrive within the hour. Three cars arrived in their ATV livery well on time to be followed, a few minutes later, by a fourth car containing the reporter. I had arranged a suitable room and there we repaired.

Within minutes the crew had its equipment assembled and we were ready. The reporter and I had been discussing the interview and its content and we had agreed that I would explain my aim and then give a few examples. The reporter, Bev Smith, then suggested that we began. I sat in a chair faced by a seemingly enormous cyclops and went through my 'act'. There were few technical hitches, but very shortly the reporter was satisfied. Bev asked me if I knew any Irish police jokes. I told him that I knew several but I would rather not particularise, anyway there were enough Irish jokes on the market. However, he persuaded me to tell him one. I explained to him the entrance qualifications for the Garda Siochana: To be an inspector you have to be able to read and write, to be a sergeant you have to be able to read or write and to be a constable you have to *know* someone who can read or write!

I went on to explain that I knew quite a few Irish police officers and I had no wish to be offensive on television. I then realised that the camerman was still active and though I was assured otherwise, I was convinced, until I saw the transmission that evening, that I had been recorded telling the Irish tale.

At the end of the interview I realised that, in fact, it had not been an interview in the normal way, more of a monologue. Apart from the little discussion at the end I had not been asked a single question. All was revealed. I was asked to sit in front of the camera again, look at some letters I had received, smoke my pipe and laugh. Bev then went in front of the camera, asked several questions and laughed a little. He explained that the film would be sent to the studios in Birmingham where it would be edited, the questions and laughter being added in the appropriate places.

The day following that episode, I received a similar invitation but this time from BBC television. Instead of the interview being recorded, though, it was to be live. The studio is in Birmingham and my office some 50 miles away in Derbyshire and it was agreed that I should be interviewed 'down the line' from Nottingham. At 3pm I had a call from Tom Coyne, the interviewer. We discussed the format of the interview and he told me it would be approximately four minutes and would be placed at the beginning of the programme which started at 5.55pm. I was asked to be in the studio at Nottingham by 5.15pm.

I arrived well in time and found the studio to be over a shop in the city centre, and that the full staff was there to greet me— lady receptionist and an engineer. I was made most welcome and at 5.25pm was seated in a pocket-sized studio faced by a remotely controlled camera. There were so many wires about I can remember thinking to myself that the whole set was like a large plateful of spaghetti. Some of the bulbs shining on me were almost the size of footballs and there must have been thirty of them. The engineer explained that they were quartz-iodine lamps and had a tendency to make one a little warm—the understatement of the year; by 5.35pm I was on the point of melting. It was about that time that I realised that everything was not quite right. The engineer, a friendly chap, explained that the line to Birmingham was 'playing-up'. Frantic conversations passed from Nottingham to Birmingham and back while the studio clock ticked on. At 5.54 pm, one minute before the beginning of transmission, it was decided to re-arrange the schedule and I was to be interviewed towards the end of the programme or, rather, before the Midlands 'patched-into' BBC 'Nationwide' at 6.20pm. The programme progressed and I began to wonder when I would be cued-in. The time was 6.18pm and the length of my interview, by arrangement was to be four minutes. That moment Tom Coyne introduced me. The very moment I began to speak, the engineer behind the camera changed from his friendly approach to a threatening stance. He was moving his right arm in a frantic circular motion, at the same time mouthing 'Speed it up, speed it up!' In what seemed little more than ten seconds, Tom was thanking me and I could see from the monitor that the viewers were now watching 'Nationwide'. I was assured afterwards that I had managed in two minutes to deliver four minutes material.

I had been warned by my colleagues of the 'under-arm' questions which some interviewers would slip-in from time to time even though, usually, the questions had been discussed and agreed beforehand. I was pleased that I was prepared at a radio interview which was being recorded. The interviewer had a reputation for his antagonistic attitude to police officers. We discussed the content at some length. I had a feeling that the interviewer would attack from the start and I was prepared. 'Superintendent Harris,' he started, 'a book about police humour must, of necessity, be a very slim volume?'

'You mean about as thin as a book of journalistic ethics?' I replied. I will give the interviewer credit, with only a small break, he continued the interview.

What I have related above are just a few stories from many which I experienced. It was a tremendously interesting time and showed that there was a sympathetic interest in the police service from the media.

## What is a policeman?

He, of all men, is at once the most needed and the most unwanted. He's a strangely nameless creature who is 'Sir' to his face and 'Pig' to his back. He must be such a diplomat that he can settle differences between individuals so that each will think he's won.

But!

If the policeman is neat, he's conceited, if he's careless, he's a bum. If he's pleasant, he's a flirt, if he's not, he's a grouch. He must make in an instant, decisions which would require months for a lawyer.

But!

If he hurries, he's careless, if he's deliberate, he's lazy. He must be first to an accident and infallible with a diagnosis. He must be able to start breathing, stop bleeding, tie splints and above all, be sure the victim goes home without a limp, or expect to be sued.

And!

A policeman must know everything and not tell. He must know where all the sin is and not partake. The policeman must, from a single human hair be able to describe the crime, the weapon and the criminal, and tell you where the criminal is hiding.

But!

If he catches the criminal, he's lucky: if he doesn't, he's a dullard. The policeman must chase bum leads to a dead end, stake out ten nights to tag one witness who saw it happen, but refuses to remember. He runs files and writes reports until his eyes ache to build a case against some felon who'll get dealt out by a shameless shamus or an 'Honourable' who isn't.

The policeman must be a minister, a social worker, a diplomat, a tough guy and a gentleman.

(Extract from an American radio broadcast)

\*     \*     \*

The following is an article which appeared in the 'Police' magazine. Its author, M. J. Hirst, Esq., is now assistant chief constable with the Lincolnshire Constabulary.

### Join the professionals

My regular readers, that is my inspector hoping to find grounds for serving me with discipline forms, and my superintendent who merely seeks an action for libel, may note an air of despondency about my contribution on this occasion. No more the happy carefree gay abandon one associates with periods of annual leave, but more the black despondency known to anyone familiar with a not guilty shoplifter defended by a QC. The worst possible event in the life of a PC has come to pass. No, not a weekend in Blackpool with the policewoman superintendent. It's even worse than that! I have been returned to shift work.

No civilian could possibly appreciate the implications of what I have just said. After 11 years of 9 to 5 duty and weekends off, plus ARD payment for only taking two tea breaks a day instead of four, I now find myself once again faced with nights, lates and earlies, wet pavements and banana sandwiches. Weekends and bank holidays have ceased to exist. I only see Kojak one week in five and I have already been reported for threatening my neighbour's children with Borstal for disturbing my daylight repose.

### Injustice

Perhaps at this point I might be allowed the luxury of describing what I euphemistically call my police career to date in order that you will be able to appreciate the injustice of what has happened.

There comes a time in every copper's life when he has to ask himself what he wants from the job. There are two choices—to remain an amateur or become a professional. The alternatives are best illustrated by the detective and the dog handler. The former working all hours being shot at, swearing his life away in the witness box; the latter home every night, four hours every day throwing sticks for his dog (except on notional rest days when he throws it for six hours) and worried about nothing more than the possibility of a hole in his wellies. The concept of amateurs and professionals separates the mere legionaries from the Praetorian Guard, patriotic TAVR's from the Mercenaries, the Monsieur Clusots from the James Bonds. The professionals first objective is to survive and this means getting out of the firing line—which brings me back to my own early career.

**Amateur**

For the first five years of my service I must admit I was an amateur—arresting people with gay abandon, stopping runaway horses with consumate ease and throwing myself in front of stolen cars like there was no tomorrow. I must have been insane. I even fancied the CID. I taught myself to speak without my lips moving, didn't buy a round for five months and ate all my meals in a dirty garberdine and pushed back trilby—all necessary traits in the potential CID man.

And then it happened, I met the legendary widow of a rich licensee with nymphaniacal tendencies (not the licensee the widow!) and what's more she had her own Jaguar. Can you imagine that, at a time when I had to walk four miles home after half nights and I couldn't afford a bike and police cars were things you only saw at the cinema. To be ferried everywhere in a 3.8 was the epitome of sophistication. Unfortunately my work began to suffer due to my continual state of mild exhaustion, due more to the nymphaniacal than to the Jaguar aspect of the relationship. I was almost killed on point duty by the back end of a tram flicking across the points which at my peak I would have avoided like a white coated Fred Astaire, and when I fell asleep on the bus going off nights and finished up in Whitby, 74 miles from my lodgings, I had to act. I decided to turn professional, relinquish my amateur status and CID aspirations and seek permanent day duties.

**Salvation**

My salvation came in Weekly Orders—'Applications are invited for a vacancy in the dog section, apply Supt. Traffic'. This was my chance for permanent days, unlimited sex, free ale and the 3.8 litre transport of delight. My cup runneth over. The selection board comprised the superintendent, the dog sergeant and two alsatians. The statutory bit of subservience, a convincing tale, and two handfuls of Cruckles and I was in, the proud owner of 'Attila the Hun' formerly a German shepherd dog, latterly the scourge of the Salvation Army Hostel Urban Terrorist Movement. But that's another story, I had joined the professionals.

Inevitably as my stamina waned, my widow grew cold. I realised that she had only wanted my virile smooth young body as a plaything. Unfortunately her head had been turned by an undermanager from Tesco who plied her with quadruple green shield stamps, and I was left with Attila. But I had grown accustomed to the decadence of permanent days and realised that my future lay in this direction.

Again providence provided the answer. I heard a whisper that the deputy chief had started breeding show rabbits. He had always been a man of the soil and the rabbits were another milestone in a long line of hobbies which had ranged from bantams and tropical fish to white mice and ferrets. He was a sort of frustrated farmer of humble origins. His father was a drainage inspector in Clitheroe and his mother the manageress of a multi-storey knackers yard in Huddersfield. Anyway, with the knowledge gleaned from two library books and armed with a few names like Tortoise Dutch, Ermine Rex and Chinchilla, I was ready. It took just nine days of lunching at headquarters conspicuously reading 'Fur and Feathers Weekly' before he spotted me. I did my usual grovelling bit, apologised profusely for lowering the tone of the place and craved his indulgence for being a mere rabbit fancier. Before I knew it I was invited round to his house. The following Monday, I spent three hours admiring funny little animals which hitherto I had only ever seen on a plate surrounded by Yorkshire pudding and covered in onion gravy. Within a week I was transferred to Headquarters as an admin. clerk and Attila was looking for a new kennel.

### Gardener

I consolidated my position by letting slip to the chief constable, a keen gardener, that my brother-in-law had his own nursery, and I was home and dry, I don't think the word indispensible would be inappropriate at this junction of my career. That my brother-in-law did not have a nursery and I bought all the chief's plants from a stall in the market is neither here nor there. The fact remains that for 11 years I was on permanent days.

Reorganisation was my undoing—that and the new chief constable we acquired. He is definitely an amateur of the first order and he rumbled me from the word go. He makes Lawrence of Arabia look like one of the three stooges. He first saw me gathering dandelions behind headquarters for the old deputy's rabbits. Two days later he caught me with four dozen mixed brassicas for the old chief. And when he found me in the Research and Planning Department grooming two Belgian Hares, I knew that my cards were marked. The following Monday I was back on digestion destruction duty after 11 years loyal service, if not to the job then to the DCC's rabbits, without so much as a QPM.

And my disappointment did not end there. I suddenly found myself surrounded by a complete shift of amateurs. I reported for my first tour of duty—nights of course—and assumed that the group of callow youths in crew neck sweaters and bell bottom jeans were visitors from the local comprehensive school —that is until they changed into uniform and paraded for nights.

### Old Guard

What's happened to the Old Guard? Where are the old sweats who wouldn't speak to you until you had a minimum of three years service? The hard cases with flasks of tea and Neanderthal expressions. The guardsmen, commando and paratroopers who marched everywhere. There is only one man on my current shift out of his probation and he's the sergeant—and I'm beginning to wonder about him.

But the worst innovation is this firearms business—definitely a sign of amateurism. Outside only four weeks and already I have been issued with a gun on two occasions. The first time was a major traffic jam which the brilliant Special Course inspector thought was a hijacking. I finished up doing three hours point duty with a Lee Enfield in one hand and a gas grenade in the other. The second time was when a bull escaped from the abattoir. We were given Browning automatics and two bullets—one for the bull and the second presumably for yourself if you missed with the first. I explained to the governor I was a national service pacifist, a member of the League against Cruel Sports and was still recovering from a vasectomy, but all to no avail. Times have changed.

### Consolation

There is only one consolation to an old professional. These pink skinned youngsters won't offer much competition when I decide to go back on permanent days. And I think I've spotted just the job—the divisional collator. Make up a few names—call it 'hard intelligence' and you're in business. What's more he shares his office with the sweetest little switchboard operator you have ever seen. She has her own flat, widow as well, and (you guessed) she has a brand new Jensen Healey. I wonder if the superintendent could use a few onion sets from my brother's non-existent nursery, or a few fresh eggs from his fictitious poultry farm. I've always said, and I still believe it, coppering's a good job if you're a Professional!

★        ★        ★

Extract from Strathclyde Guardian:

## CLAIMS CLANGERS

The following are actual statements found on insurance forms where car drivers attempted to summarise the details of an accident in the fewest possible words. The instances of faulty writing serve to confirm that even incompetent writing may be highly entertaining:

Coming home I drove into the wrong house and collided with a tree I don't have.

The other car collided with mine without giving warning of its intention.

I thought the window was down, but found it was up when I put my head through it.

I collided with a stationary truck coming the other way.

A truck backed through my windshield into my wife's face.

A pedestrian hit me and went under the car.

The guy was all over the road, I had to swerve a number of times before I hit him.

I pulled away from the side of the road, glanced at my mother-in-law and headed over the embankment.

In an attempt to kill a fly, I drove into a telephone pole.

I had been shopping for plants all day and was on my way home. As I approached an intersection a hedge sprang up, obscuring my vision and I did not see the other car.

I had been driving for 40 years when I fell asleep at the wheel and had an accident.

I was on my way to the doctor with rear end trouble when my universal joint gave way causing me to have an accident.

As I approached the intersection a sign suddenly appeared in a place where no stop sign had ever appeared before. I was unable to stop in time to avoid the accident.

To avoid hitting the bumper of the car in front I struck a
pedestrian.

My car was legally parked as it backed into the other vehicle.
An invisible car came out of nowhere, struck my car and
vanished.

I told the police that I was not injured, but on removing my
hat found that I had a fractured skull.

I was sure that the old fellow would never make it to the other
side of the road when I struck him.

The pedestrian had no idea which direction to run, so I ran
over him.

I saw a slow moving, sad faced old gentleman as he bounced
off the roof of my car.

The indirect cause of the accident was a little guy in a small
car with a big mouth.

*     *     *

# METROPOLITAN POLICE OFFICE

### Public Orders
Thursday, December 20, 1860

**Caution against drinking**

The commissioner feels it necessary at this season to repeat
the caution given on former occasions against any excess of
drinking by the police. Any constable reported for
drunkenness is not to be allowed to go on duty again, but is
to be suspended at once by the superintendent until he can be
brought before the commissioner. All must refrain from
taking drink offered to them on duty, and remember that no
excuse can be allowed for any man who renders himself
unequal to the performance of his duty by drinking. After
this caution, any man reported for drinking will have no
plea against being punished by dismissal. This Order is to be
ready daily to the men, and each superintendent is to adopt
all precautionary arrangements to give effect to it.

**Whiskers and hair to be properly cut**

Several of the police have been noticed whose whiskers are
so long as to hide the numbers on their coat collars.

Superintendents are to observe all such cases, and direct the men to have their whiskers and hair properly cut, so as to appear smart and clean, and not to come down upon the collar of the coat.

## Testimonial to Superintendent Branford (M)
The commissioner has much pleasure in allowing Superintendent Branford to receive a valuable timepiece and a diamond ring, presented to him by several inhabitants of Rotherhithe, as a testimonial for his straightforward conduct in connection with his official duties, and also for having introduced various measures of improvement for the police of the division under his control, which has given great satisfaction.

\*       \*       \*

## R. T. M. Henry, MVO, OBE, QPM, CPM
## Hong Kong Police
### Efficiency of investigations
Some years ago in the Royal Hong Kong Police there was a senior officer who was renowned for his pernickety attitude towards his subordinates' work. He was also well known for hastily skimming through his in-tray and not giving all the attention to its contents that he should have.

One day he picked up an investigation paper which dealt with the unfortunate sudden death of a very inebriated gentlemen who had staggered out of a drinking place late on a wet and rainy night, tripped on the pavement and had fallen face down in a puddle. Tragically the cause of death was inhalation of rainwater which had caused the pathologist to certify death by drowning.

The busy senior officer skipped through the investigation paper and read only the pathologist's report, then, with great panache, he minuted the file back to the investigating officer saying 'I note the cause of death is drowning but I can see no mention on this file as to whether or not the deceased could swim'.

Some weeks later the same investigating officer was allocated a case of suicide in which the deceased had jumped to his death from a tall building. History does not relate whether he was playing absolutely safe or whether he was taking the proverbial mickey, but he ended his summary of facts for submission of the papers to his superior with the sentence 'It should be noted that the deceased could not fly'.

*     *     *

Letter from solicitor:
Dear Sir,

### Re Accident

We thank you for your letter of 13th June, 1980, the contents of which are noted. The accident occurred at approximately 4.45pm on the A38 road. Our client was riding a Suzuki Sport motorbike. He was travelling in the general direction of Derby.

The accident occurred when our client was hit by a cat's eye which had been dislodged by a vehicle travelling in the opposite direction. We understand that the cat's eye is now in the possession of the Derbyshire Constabulary, although we do not know the name of the reporting officer.

Our client was taken to the Derbyshire Royal Infirmary where he gave a statement to a police officer.

We trust that this information will be sufficient to assist you in tracing the accident report and we await hearing from you in due course.

Yours faithfully,

*     *     *

**Extract from Strathclyde Guardian**

### A Fair Cop

The following letter was received as a clipping from an unidentified British newspaper:

State of Maine v David P Cons

Dear Mr Cons,

Your letter of October 19th, 1979, to the Clerk of the Sixth District Court in Bath, Maine, was referred to me by the judge of the court for response and resolution of the case. The officer is as adamant that you were speeding as you are that you were not, which necessitates a trial on the merits of the case.

The options that are available to you are as follows: The first is that you fly to the United States and appear for the trial, a most unlikely choice.

The second is that you retain counsel in the United States, waive your presence at the trial, in which case you would be tried in absentia and most likely found guilty. The fine for this matter would be $30.

The third possibility that you plead guilty and pay the fine of $30.

Both of these options would be beneficial to the State of Maine in that they would have a noticeable and salutary effect upon our balance of trade deficit here in the United States. The last option that is available to you is to do nothing, in which case a default will be entered against you and a warrant will be issued for your arrest.

This leaves several options available to me: the first is to have you arrested in England and arrange for your extradition. This would take approximately two years and cost the County of Sagahadoc no less than $3,000. The second option available would be to move for a change of venue (by permission of the court) and try your case in the Old Bailey. This is by far the preferable option, I have several very fine local defense attorneys and one local judge who would be more than delighted to join me in London to try this matter. The cost to the County of Sagahadoc and the State of Maine in this option would be totally irrelevant.

My last option, of course, would be to dismiss the case altogether. After reviewing all the available alternatives, I have decided that I will have to overlook the better interest of the Secretary of the Treasury and my wife's travel desires, and exercise this last option. I consider this another stone in the foundation of Anglo-American solidarity.

I hope that you had a good trip to the United States, and that you return in the future. I also hope that if and when you do return, you remember to drive slowly in the State of Maine.

*       *       *

It used to be called Civil Defence; it is now called Home Defence and the police, together with other essential services, continue to be trained in preparing for their responsibilities in the event of a nuclear attack. The following two tales concern this subject.

Advice to police officers in the event of an impending nuclear attack: 'Dig a hole 18 feet by 18 feet by six feet deep. Climb into the hole with as many people as possible and cover yourselves with the soil taken out of the hole. This action will not give you a protective factor, but at least you will be satisfied that you have left the place neat and tidy!'

Amongst other things, it is impressed upon police officers receiving Home Defence training that, once the device has been exploded, they should keep under cover until the gamma radiation outside has fallen sufficiently for them to emerge without danger to themselves. Once it is safe to venture forth they should make contact with other members of the public and their colleagues and follow plans already formulated.

Hostilities between the major blocs were imminent. There had been a deterioration in relationships over a period of several months and each side had gone over to a war footing. Eventually it happened, the four-minute warning was received and, eventually the holocaust.

Fourteen days passed and Constable Jones pushed open the door of his fall-out shelter. Checking with his radiac instrument he found that the radiation was at a minimum, so he opened the door further. He looked around, there was devastation everywhere. As far as the eye could see there was not one building standing; no trees, no telegraph poles, nothing.

He remembered his training—he must make contact with someone else. He started by searching in the immediate vicinity but it was soon obvious that there was no-one about. If only he could find a telephone! There was not one to be found. He decided that he must make his way to police headquarters, some five miles away. He found it difficult making his way through the rubble but he eventually arrived at the site where the headquarters had originally stood—just another pile of rubble. It was the same everywhere, flattened buildings and no-one to be seen. For a few hours he sat and thought. Surely he wasn't the only survivor. He must spread his search further afield. During the next few weeks he travelled the whole of the county without success. He had found a few basic items for human survival, uncontaminated food and water, extra clothing and a bicycle which he could use where roads remained undamaged. He was undeterred, his search must go on to find someone else. It seemed now that, to ensure the continuance of humanity he had to meet up with someone else.

Months passed into years as he travelled the four corners of this country in his search. Everywhere the picture was exactly the same, complete devastation and no sign of life.

The spirit was still alive in Constable Jones. He could have been excused for giving up, but the pervisity of human nature was such that, instead of being despondent, he was even further committed in his task. He made his way to Dover and, eventually, found a small boat. He ensured there was sufficient fuel and set off for France. As soon as he landed on the beach his fears were confirmed—the countryside revealed exactly the scene he had become accustomed to in the United Kingdom. His search of France and other countries in Europe was more perfunctory than in the UK and he travelled on and on. He went through Russia and saw that the retaliation had been as thorough as the initial attack. The sub-continent of India had not escaped nor had Malaysia. In Singapore Jones found himself an ocean-going boat he could manage and he set sail. Australia was no different from what he had found elsewhere. Time had no meaning to Jones he travelled on. Some 10 years had passed since the nuclear holocaust and he found himself in San Francisco, no buildings standing, no people. The same was so of the rest of the United States—until he arrived in New York. There he found that there was massive devastation, he had become used to that, there was no-one to be seen, that was a familiar picture too. The difference was that the Empire State Building was still standing intact. With difficulty Jones made his way through the remains of the city towards the one complete building he had seen in years. If the building was intact there surely must be some life somewhere. Jones' training had taught him to contact other survivors, was he about to achieve this? He entered the building and searched every office, floor by floor. Almost exhausted he reached the top floor, but every office had been empty.

This was too much; he'd had enough. For years Jones had been trying to find someone else. He had travelled the world but he had failed. There was nothing left for him to do. He opened a window, looked out on the empty street beneath and jumped. He fell rapidly towards the roadway, and his death. As he passed the twentieth floor he heard the telephone ring!

*    *    *

Returning home at 2.00 am from a Rugby Dinner/Dance a man discovered that he had left his key in the house before leaving. Not to worry he had his car and garage keys and there was a ladder in the garage. He gave the matter some thought and went to the kiosk at the street corner and rang the local police station to let them know that he was going to enter his house using a ladder just in case someone mistook him for a breaker. The station sergeant listened sympathetically, offered to send a patrol car if the man couldn't manage to climb in the bedroom window, thanked him for his consideration and foresight and wished him goodnight.

Just as the man was putting his leg into the bedroom window some five minutes later, a police car came skidding around the corner—'just checking!'

*     *     *

A lady had parked her car in town while she went shopping. She and her husband knew that the tyres were coming towards the end of their legal life and had taken the car to the local discount garage for new front tyres. The garage did not have the size but agreed to order them and fit them on the day following the incident about to be related. After shopping, the lady returned to her car to find a very young policeman kneeling down, notebook in hand, at the front of the car looking intently at the tyres.

The lady had two choices, she could either walk past pretending it was nothing to do with her or else face the music. She chose the latter, and with what she hoped was a beaming smile greet him: 'Good afternoon officer, I hope nothing is wrong?'

He stood up, but was still remarkably short for a policeman, and he said: 'I have to inform you that these front tyres are illegal.' The lady talked—how she talked—she told him the story of the visit to the garage and the following day's appointment. This did not move him at all, and he, quite rightly, pointed out that there was more than one place to buy tyres. She agreed, but pointed out that on her budget she preferred the discount garage.

He did not seem to appreciate this, and added that as both front tyres were under the limit she would be liable to two fines and two endorsements. She panicked and found herself talking off the top of her head, saying: 'Well as my husband and I both have clean licences, please can we have one each?' He swallowed hard—not with supressed amusement even though she thought she had been terribly witty, and told her that if he ever saw that particular car with those particular tyres again he would jump on it from a great height. He crossed out the entry in his

notebook and walked away from the shabby car, leaving the
lady with knocking knees and a complete inability to swallow.

*     *     *

Returning from the cinema one evening a young lady alighted
from the 'bus in Onslow Square, in London, and walked
towards the block of flats where she lived. En route she noticed
three men creeping around a large house on the Square. One
seemed to be looking into a ground floor window! She passed
quickly and upon reaching home, decided that she should be
public spirited and so she duly telphoned the police telling them,
in a breathless manner, all she had seen.

Within an hour she was visited by a most courteous officer
who thanked her for her help, but pointed out that the men were
plainclothes policemen about to raid a gaming party!

*     *     *

This is an old tale. Some 50 years ago when oil lamps were used
on cycles, a lady was cycling along the promenade in
Cheltenham when the cycle jerked over a bump in the road
extinguishing the oil light. Out stepped a police officer who
accused the lady of riding without a light.

The constable would not believe her about the bump and, to
prove his point he put his hand on the top of the lamp. You can
imagine what happened. The constable screamed out in pain
and left a goodly portion of skin from his palm on the top of the
lamp.

*     *     *

The following is a precis from an article in the 'Carmarthen
Journal'. It was the report of proceedings at a magistrates'
court. The paper reported the policeman's statement to the
court: 'I was on my beat walking down towards the Towy
Bridge, when I saw someone who appeared to be urinating over
the bridge. When he turned round I saw it was—John Thomas.'

*     *     *

A young constable rang the station in the early hours of the
morning to inform the station sergeant that there was a lion on
his beat. After a few words the youngster insisted that he was
not drunk, not mad, fully in command of his senses and that the
lion was still there in the doorway. The station sergeant ordered
ropes, chains, nets, gloves and a gun and sent three men to the

spot in question in a van. They arrived, met the constable, worked out the plan and approached the doorway in question, shone a bright light into the doorway. There was a fine Chow dog just waiting to be let into the house. The constable never lived it down; thereafter being called 'Tiger'.

*      *      *

Soon after the second world war many ex-servicemen joined the police service. Joining the same force on the same day were two men. One was smallish, thin and studious, and the other very large with a fresh complexion. They were immediately nick-named Brain and Brawn. Somewhile later they were both sent to the same incident to assist officers already there. A man had committed suicide by putting his head in the gas oven. They were detailed to inspect the kitchen and return with a sketch plan. A simple exercise but the result was hilarious.

After an hour or so they returned enthusiastically asked for graph paper. After much deliberation they got the wall lengths and square footage correct. They inserted the back door, the communicating door and the window. Then they came unstuck.

'Where was the sink?' said Brain.

'Behind the door,' replied Brawn.

'Which door?' queried Brain.

'Why, the back door, of course,' snorted Brawn.

'I thought the table was behind the back door,' stated Brian.

'No the table was under the window,' sighed Brawn.

'The mangle was under the window,' replied Brain.

'The mangle was in the yard,' yelled Brawn.

'The sink must have been behind the other door then,' ruminated Brain.

'Couldn't have been,' said Brawn, 'because that door opened outwards. Got to be opening inwards for anything to be behind it!'

'Well, where was the sink then?' demanded Brain.

'Oh, I'm past caring!' exclaimed Brawn. 'After all he put his head in a gas oven. He didn't drown himself!!!'

Brawn had obviously had enough.

Brain kept studying the plan, pondered a while and then, in a very calm voice, asked the impossible:

'Where *was* the gas oven, by the way?'

In the police service, perhaps, more than in any other occupation it is necessary to retain a sense of humour if only to stem the suicidal fits of depression which can come on when we see how the other half lives. A policeman's humour, therefore, is drawn more often than not from real life situations in which he finds himself and which he is eager to recount to his colleagues at the first opportunity. A good example follows:

The scene was the Police Room at Ibrox Park on 1st January, and as the door burst open two very hot young constables dragged in a semicomatose drunk who was built along the lines of th Q.E.II. With their last ounce of strength the constables pulled the prisoner along the floor and in doing so his trousers descended to his ankles revealing a bare backside which an elephant would have been proud to own.

At this point a second prisoner was brought into the room who was screaming, kicking, punching and biting to such an extent that the drunk was left lying on the floor face down and bottom up while all hands went to quiten the madman.

This was the scene which met the eyes of the sergeant when he entered. There was the huge backside together with the terrible cacophany. It was too much for him 'What's this?' he said, 'are they trying to do a remake of 'Jaws?''

                                                                *T. M. Frood*

*            *            *

**Humour at court**
John was no stranger to the court having appeared before the magistrate on numerous occasions on charges of disorder. It was, therefore, no surprise when he was once again sentenced to a period of 30 days' imprisonment.

While being escorted from the dock, determined to have the last word and no doubt still suffering the effects of over indulgence, he was heard to shout in the direction of the bench, 'I can do that standing on my hands'.

On hearing this the magistrate ordered that John be returned to the dock whereupon he imposed a further sentence of 30 days' imprisonment for contempt of court. This had a very sobering effect on poor John as did the magistrate's parting remarks, 'That will give you time to get back on your feet'.

*            *            *

When Parliament dissolves for the summer break, and their Lordships repair to the grouse-moors, a dearth of news seems to result. Newspaper editors have christened this period the 'silly season' for they have to scratch around for items to titilate their readers until the 'hard' news begins again. The 'silly season' seemed to arrive in Accrington in October. It all started when the Prosecutions Department issued a summons to a gentleman for commiting an offence in Inner Relief Road, Rawtenstall. Would you believe the offence was urinating?

Similarly a constable visited a house in Oswaldtwhistle to report the sudden death of an elderly gentleman and inquired of the relatives if the deceased had been ailing much recently. He was told: 'Nay lad, he hasn't been out for a pint for over six months now!'

\*        \*        \*

From time to time typographical errors are to be seen in the best of publications. Not always are they corrected, and when they are the correction occasionally makes things no better. The following was recently noted in a professional publication. 'Suggestion for stuffing the Inspectorate will be passed on immediately.' In the ensueing edition there appeared a short apologetic paragraph which went on to inform readers that it should have read: 'Suggestions for staffing the Inspectorate will be p.ssed on immediately.'

\*        \*        \*

Traffic Bulletin: The detour signs will be conspicuously placed so that no-one will have any trouble getting lost.

\*        \*        \*

At a court at Lancaster several prosecutions came one after the other for driving a motor without due care and attention and in each case the defendant was fined and his licence was endorsed. Then came a pedal-cyclist charged with riding his cycle without due care and attention. The magistrate leaned over to the prosecuting inspector and said: 'Well, inspector, I can hardly endorse his licence'. As quick as a flash the inspector replied: 'No sir, but you could confiscate his bicycle clips!'

\*        \*        \*

The policeman stood at the gates of Heaven
His head was bent and low,
He meekly asked the man at the gate,
The way that he should go.

St. Peter asked, 'What have you done
'To gain admission here?'
He said: 'I've been a copper down below
'For many and many a year.'

St. Peter opened wide the gates
And gently pressed the bell
'Come inside, and choose your harp,
'You've had your share of hell!'

*      *      *

A complaint was received at the Darwen Police Station:
To the inspector

Darwen Police are very thick,
And a lad on York Avenue is very quick,
All he does in just relax,
And drives a car round with no tax.

Panda cars come up here often,
He just sits about there and doesn't soften,
For he knows beyond a doubt,
Left to the Police he can drive about.

Signed—Observer

The letter was received by the chief inspector who forwarded it
to the section sergeant for action by adding the following:

This letter was most uncomplimentary
Requires action elementary,
Though in dreadful rhyme it is composed,
Report for any offence disclosed.

The action was taken and report submitted for process with
the following added:

With reference to the above,
I report that I'm no dove,
Observations have been kept,
I've caught this chap within my net,
As PCs we may be thick,

But this lad is not so quick,
No longer does he relax,
And drives his car without tax,
For he knows beyond a doubt,
He can't relax when we're about.

Forwarded to divisional headquarters the superintendent added the following:

On reading this ridiculous rhyme,
I considered the waste of police time,
And therefore checked the discipline code,
In case reg.4 covered the drafting of an ode.

But, being the festive season, this in part,
Made me have a change of heart.

I compliment the Darwen Section,
For their prompt and effective action,
Lastly, to bring this matter to conclusion,
I now authorise a prosecution.

★        ★        ★

In the middle of a summer night a gang of thieves broke into a warehouse and stole a lorry load of carpets. They were disturbed before they could make their getaway, and they and their lorry were chased into the courtyard of a block of flats. The flats were surrounded by police and the villains were trapped, obviously hiding out in one of the flats. The inspector in charge sent for a dog. The trail was fresh and the dog would be able to track from the lorry to the flat in which the thieves were hiding. There was a short calm while the policemen awaited the arrival of the handler and his trusty friend. Soon the sound of a siren on an approaching police car. It swung into the yard with its headlights full on, the blue lamp flashing, and the tyres screeching. The dog handler leapt out.

'Stand back,' he ordered, 'stand well back. He's vicious on the trail'—and he flung the back door open.

No dog at all. He'd left him up to the ears in munchy morsels at the police station.

For years after he couldn't see the funny side, and would turn quite nasty if anyone shouted 'Stand back, he's vicious' when he came into the canteen.

*     *     *

**Extract from 'Round the Horne', written by Barry Took & Marty Feldman, and first broadcast on BBC Radio on 20th February, 1967**
Sung to the tune 'Clementine'
Rambling Syd Rumpo (Kenneth Williams)

> Joe he was a young cordwangler,
> Monging greebles did he go,
> And he loved a bogler's daughter
> By the name of Chiswick Flo.

> Vain she was and like a grusset,
> Though her ganderparts were fine—
> But she sneered at his cordwangle
> As it hung upon the line.

> So he stole a wogglers moulie,
> For to make a wedding ring—
> But the Bow Street Runners caught him
> And the judge said he will swing.

> Oh they hung him by the postern,
> Nailed his moulie to the fence—
> For to warn all young cordwanglers
> That it was a grave offence.

> There's a moral in this story
> Though your cordwangle be poor—
> Keep your hands off others moulies,
> For it is against the law. Oh!

*     *     *

### Ode to the Demon Drink

The horse and cow live 30 thirty years, and nothing know of wines and beers.
The goat and sheep at 20 die, and never taste of scotch and rye.
The sow drinks water by the ton, and at 18 is nearly done.

The dog at 15 cashes in, without the aid of rum or gin.
The cat, in milk and water soaks, and then, at 12 short years it croaks.
The modest sober, bone-dry hen, lays her eggs for years, and dies at 10.
All animals are strictly dry, they sinless live and swiftly die.
But sinful, ginful, rum-soaked men, survive for three score years and ten.
And some of us . . . the mighty few, stay pickled till we're 92.

*          *          *

Humour is odd, grotesque and wild,
Only by affectation spoiled.
'Tis never by invention got,
Men have it when they know it not.
Johnathan Swift 1667-1745

*          *          *

Wise men plead causes,
but fools decide them.

Plutarch

*          *          *

A policeman goes after vice as an officer of the law and comes away as a philosopher.

Finley Peter Dunne
'Mr Dooley Remembers'

*          *          *

And hungry judges soon the sentence sign,
And wretches hang that jurymen may dine.
Alexander Pope

*          *          *

The difference between a lawyer and a solicitor
is simply that of a crocodile and an alligator.

Anon

*          *          *

There is a general prejudice to the effect that lawyers are more honourable than politicians but less honourable than prostitutes. This is an exaggeration.

Alexander King
'Rich Man, Poor Man, Freud and Fruit'

'My Lord,' said the foreman of an Irish jury when giving in his verdict, 'we find the man who stole the mare not guilty.'

*          *          *

For several years I have lectured on Appreciation and Planning to inspectors prior to their attendance at the Police Staff College. One morning, after returning from coffee, I found on the lectern on top of my notes the following notice:

### Notice

The objective of all dedicated officers within the police service should be to analyse thoroughly all situations, anticipate all problems prior to their occurrence, have answers for these problems, and move swiftly to resolve them when called upon... However . . . when you are up to your backside in alligators, it is difficult to remind yourself that your initial objective was to drain the swamp!

*          *          *

Displayed on Divisional Notice Board:

### Table of excuses
To save everyone's time
give your excuse by number

 1. That's the way we've always done it.
 2. I didn't know you were in a hurry for it.
 3. That's not in my department/division/section.
 4. No one told me to go ahead.
 5. I'm waiting for an OK.
 6. How did I know this was different?
 7. That's his job—not mine!
 8. Wait till the inspector comes back and ask him.
 9. I was on leave.
10. It was my twin brother.
11. I forgot.
12. I didn't think it was very important.
13. I'm so busy I just can't get around to it!
14. I thought I told you.
15. I wasn't hired to do that!
16. I'm not happy about the walls!
17. I'm not bothered.
18. I just don't wanna talk about it!
19. I just can't cope.

# HUMOUR AND THE POLICE REVIEW

The Police Review has served the police service for many, many years as its weekly magazine. In many areas it helps the dissemination of all aspects of police life. Through its columns members of the service and the staff associations make their views known; it also has its educational content. Apart from its very professional approach it occasionally allows itself a light-hearted tilt at the service, its officers and its men.

### Spike Milligan
There are two species of Briton—those for the police and those against. I'm one of the fors. That's why I'm writing this article for a fraction of my normal fee! (You fool Milligan).

I'm suggesting that pro-police citizens should be allowed four free crimes a year:

(1) One egg allowed to be thrown at a politician of one's own choice.
(2) Kicking any Iranian student in the backside.
(3) All-day parking on a double yellow line outside the Bunny Club.
(4) A free raspberry at any member of the Royal Family— for grouse shooting.

First the funnies: true police stories of old England. A rainy night in London, traffic snarled up in Leicester Square. Traffic lights broken down—lone policeman trying to sort it out. Me desperate to find a parking place. As I drew level with a bobby I said 'Officer, do you know a good place to park?' His reply: 'Sweden.'

And again, what police force addresses the highest to the lowest with equanimity? In Bayswater (Saudi-Bayswater) a wretched Scots football drunk lying in the gutter reeking from every orifice and sick all over him, is addressed by a police officer as 'Sir'.

Another occasion: having traced a dog that fouled the pavement. I reported it to the Harrow Police Station. I was informed that 'One of our officers has cautioned the animal'.

Peter Sellers in his black Mercedes dressed as an SS officer, with me in the back done up as Hitler. Sellers sees a young PC fresh from Hendon, pulls nigh and asks him 'Zer, excuse me please officer, but vere iss zer Cherman Embassy?' 'I'm sorry Sir, I'm a stranger round here.' Touche!

I don't know why people in our cities don't take more advantage of our bobbies. No one ever seems to talk to them, except tourists. When I see a bobby on the beat or outside some forbidding embassy—I always try and have a word with him. Of course, I've had my moments . . .

Peter Sellers, always a gadget maniac had a device in his flat that connected with the Highgate Police Station. It was an innocent-looking button that hung above the bed like a light switch. While he was away on tour I had reason to sleep in his bedroom. In bed reading, I pressed what I thought was a light switch. Five minutes later what looked like the front row of the police rugby team burst in one me. It took 'phone calls, explanations, and swearing on the Bible before they released me.

The same week I was working late writing a deadline script, three in the morning, gasping for a fag. Desperate, I go to Peter Sellers' dustbin (I know he leaves dog-ends three inches long). The beam from a policeman's torch illuminates me on my knees gibbering with nicotine, crowing and grubbing in the rubbish, 'Mr Raffles, I presume?' says the constable.

Of course, I've met police villains who are in it for a punch-up. An inspector called to an 'affray' at Hammersmith gave me a truncheon, invited me to come along and 'join in'.

Another one: rugby, I was playing wing three-quarters for 'D' Battery, 56 Heavy Field Regiment, RA. We played the Sussex Police, I shall never forget the sight of 15 policemen, all 16 stone, with hair growing on their foreheads; they invoked a fear that made our 17 stone lock forward, Tiny Vicar, say 'I'm not playing them till I hear the buggers talk'.

To the Irish police, I was in a small Irish country town—the wife had gone into a shop to fill the Thermos when a tall polis' man approached.

'You can't park dere Sur,' he said.

'I won't be a second officer—I'm not obstructing any traffic.' That someone had talked back overwhelmed him. He paled, frowned, coughed and started again.

'Did ye not hear me den? You can't park here.' I explained I wouldn't be more than a minute. I was a tourist etc. He stood thunder struck—tears welled up in his eyes—then with desperation in his voice he said 'Fer God's sake drive on man,' and ran away.

Again, cheeky-bugger-police. I am driving on the M1 and to my horror I hear the police siren. A police car waves me down. What was it? Was it that girl's bicycle saddle I felt in 1939? The kid's money box? A tall elegant policeman says 'You were doing 80, Sir.'

'It wasn't me officer—it was the car.'

'Just give us your autograph, Sir.' End of chase.

Turning to the serious side of the police—I am very much aware how the force has escalated in importance since the war—there was a time when both the crime world and the police, by an unwritten law, forbade firearms. Alas those days are gone.

Despite the fact that policemen on the beat are unarmed, one has the feeling that a bobby patrolling at night would feel much safer were he armed: such is the effect of thugs who have taken to carry firearms, and 'we're going to save the world' lunatic revolutionaires (the current crop of Arabs), who are into street and embassy killings in a big way.

I would like to pose the question, how do they get arms into the country? While an Englishman can be imprisoned for carrying one, it seems incoming foreigners get them with impunity. Isn't it time that the Diplomatic Bag was subject to X-ray scrutiny? It would not affect secret documents—and it would suppress the trade in illegal firearms.

I reflect that not many professions are as arduous and dedicated as the police. At any time of the day or night an ordinary British bobby can be confronted with an armed man— people like the SAS get special pay for that sort of confrontation, I wish the public could be more aware of the every-day risk that the average bobby takes.

I was one of those saddened at the split that took place during the hippy flower power era—it has its hang-over with punk v black youths today.

I remember a confrontation at the Notting Hill Carnival between police and crowd. An angry copper shouted: 'All right, next time you're having your head bashed in—don't call a copper—call a punk.' It summed up the police's frustration point in contemporary society.

Police accept frustrations at the citizen level—but many a policeman must bang his head against the wall when, having grabbed and arrested a thug for, say, beating up a senior citizen, some looney magistrate give the accused three months at some detention centre where he learns to plant roses (and go home for week-ends).

Confidence in judges and magistrates must be at an all-time low in the light of recent judgments. I know of a case of a brutal sadistic rape attack (not the first): the man got nine years—with remission he will be out in five. I remember the police officer's face as he heard the sentence. I thought he would burst into Gilbert and Sullivan's 'A policeman's lot is not a happy one'. But what would we do without you?

★    ★    ★

## HILLIARD'S HELPFUL HINTS
## KEEPING OBSERVATION

DO NOT wear dark glasses. Dark glasses do not make you invisible. In most circumstances in which you might wish to be inconspicuous, opposite the local brothel, inside the unlicensed gaming club, at a meeting of the Nazis against Nazis Campaign, dark glasses will have the same effect as nudism at Trooping the Colour: you will be noticed. Likewise the three piece suit. The t.p.s. is commonly worn by CID officers and the type of stockbroker from whom it would be unwise to buy a second hand share; any ponce followed by a character in a three piece suit and sunglasses will not assume that he has become the sex object of a homosexual city gent with weak eyes. He will sus you out.

There is a school of disguise which favours the standard workman's outfit: overalls, flat cap, and pipe. All very well for static observation, the less movement with overalls, cap and pipe, the more natural the appearance. There are limitations to its usefulness when the suspect pops in to a mixed sauna, or decides to take the evening pink gin in the bar of the Scunthorpe Hilton. In fact there are limitations to all disguises. I once thought I had cracked the problem when I was gainfully occupied chasing street bookmakers. But I was spotted. 'How did you know?' I asked the bookie when I finally caught up with him. 'S'easy,' he said, 'yer shoes done it. Only bleeding coppers are mean enough to use stick-on soles.'

★      ★      ★

## A Cop
### by Ann S. Anderson

A cop is a human being (in the loosest meaning of the term). He comes in various sizes. If you try to pass his chair in the lounge he is of gargantuan proportions. If you want him to do a chore around the house where height would be an advantage he becomes so small he disappears.

*

A cop is found everywhere. In the kitchen, in your bed, in your bath, and in front of your dressing table—using the deodorant spray probably. He can't be found when your mother comes to tea, when the lights have fused, and when you are in the advanced stages of labour.

*

A cop can remember in the minutest detail the criminal record of every hook in the area but he can't remember his dental appointment, your birthday, how to spell your maiden name, and whom he has invited to supper tonight.

*

A cop knows where to find the loot from the latest housebreaking, the prisoner who has broken from his escort, and the owner of every stray dog. He does not know where to find scissors, his clean shirt, or today's newspaper.

*

A cop can't get time off to take his wife shopping, visit the kids in hospital, or go to his Auntie Mary's funeral. He can get time off to go fishing, watch the World Cup, and go to the police smoker.

*

A cop rarely appears at mealtimes, but he likes and expects his food to be freshly cooked and on the table the minute he comes in the door.

A cop's salary can't stretch to buying new curtains for the bedroom or a new teapot but is always sufficient to buy a fishing rod, new golf clubs, and the latest car of his desire.

*

A cop likes a warm bed to come home to from the nightshift, endless cups of coffee, having his boots cleaned for him, and dead silence when he is dozing in front of the television—switched on, of course.

*

A cop doesn't like bank statements, the last two weeks of the salary month, unforseen overtime, cancelled leave, and filing personal papers.

*

A cop is generous with criticism, scoldings, and dirty socks. He is not generous with praise, cigarettes, or help in the house.

*

However the ultimate reward for uncomplaining service to this rare specimen of manhood comes one night at 11 o'clock when, half dead from slaving over a hot typewriter all day and a hot stove all evening you are ready to fall into a hot bath, he comes in followed by Jim and Fred—and maybe even Tom and Dick—and says: 'I've brought the boys for a bite to eat. You'll manage to cook something for them won't you?' (That's his way of saying 'You're a good wife and I love you'—And you love him too.)

*       *       *

### Whitehall, a bit of a legend
Brian Hilliard

One of the many police myths that could easily be disproved if anyone were unsentimental enough to go grubbing around for the real facts is that of the PC posted to the passage leading from Horseguards Parade to Whitehall.

It was the custom at Cannon Row Police Station for many years (older, less sober PCs will swear that it was from the turn of the century) to post a constable at the end of the passage that leads from Horseguards Parade into Whitehall. His only duty appeared to be to remain at this spot until relieved.

He moved no-one on, cautioned no-one, and rarely got an opportunity to exercise his powers of arrest. Then, with the advent of one of the many inquiries into the use of police manpower, this particular posting was examined and traced back through decades of duty sheets and superintendent's memos.

It was found that an MP making his way through this passage to a late sitting of the House, brushed against the newly whitewashed wall and smudged his seven and sixpence worth of Harris tweed.

He obviously had a moan to the Home Secretary, who mentioned it to the commissioner who brought it to the attention of the local chief superintendent who promptly posted a PC to warn other hurrying MPs against the consequences of stumbling against the passage wall.

In due course the whitewash dried, the sergeant asked the inspector if they needed to continue the posting, the inspector brought it up with the chief superintendent who wasn't going to get in the red with the commissioner by consulting him over such a trivial matter, so decided to play safe and keep the posting.

A similar thing happened with the Sunday morning patrols that used to be posted from surrounding divisions to Petticoat Lane Market.

The patrols had been instituted during the war to check on the identity cards of the deserters and black marketeers who flourished there. The end of the war and the withdrawal of the identity card made no impact on the Metropolitan Police who continued to supply extra police to the market.

In 1978 with the advent of the racial disturbances centred on the Pakistani population of the area, the patrols were increased considerably, and in 1999 an inspector, two sergeants and 20 PCs will still be posted to the area on a Sunday morning without the slightest idea of the origin of their function.


**Army Version**

Those of you with experience of the armed forces will have come across other versions of the Whitehall legend. The most familiar is that of the Artillery regiment with teams of six men to each gun.

A newly transferred officer watched the teams at practice one day, and noticed that one member stood at ease throughout the operation, taking no apparent part in it.

'Sergeant,' he said, 'that man there, number six, what does he do?'

'Sir,' said the sergeant, 'number six sir, at the word of command, moves four paces to the right on a line extending from the centre of the axle of the gun wheel. He then comes to attention, sir, and marches four paces in reverse. Then he stands at ease, sir.'

'Yes, sergeant I do see all that but what does he do?'

'Do sir? Well he just stands there, sir. At ease.'

'I see,' said the thoroughly mystified officer. Later in the mess he asked his brother officers who did not know either: 'Always had a number six. Stands about seven o'clock of the cannon. Usually a smart chap. Always stands there.'

Eventually the officer tracked down the oldest serving soldier in his den at the back of the stores.

'Number six. Sir? Yes remember it well. Stands at the corner. Well, sir, when the guns was pulled by horses, number six held their reins, but when he was mobilised and there weren't no more horses, they forgot to take number six away. So he just stands there. Sir. At ease.'

Of course that's got nothing to do with the police, but it's very like it, isn't it?

*       *       *

## OUR COP

We hear a lot about school liaison from the police point of view. This is what the kids think . . . By Anne Bryson.

*

'Someone's pinched our telly,' was the greeting comment as I entered the classroom. Indeed, there was no television set in the corner. From the opposite side of the room a cold draught blew in through a broken window. 'They smashed the windows to get in and steal it,' explained a helpful six year old. It seemed he could be right.

Two policemen came to look at our vacant corner. Not much to see really. Our cleaner had thoughtfully cleared away the broken glass round the window. I don't think the policemen were too impressed with her, but they were very polite about it. While they stood about looking busy, 50 children watched them in awed silence. Suddenly a voice was raised saying, 'I know 'im, ee's Peter the policeman. Eee cums up our street.'

One of the uniformed men smiled. He was Peter Jackson, Harrington's own policeman, visiting Harrington Infant's School.

When Peter and his colleague left, two fingerprint men arrived. They weren't quite so interesting as the uniformed men, although the children preferred watching them to doing their work. It was not a normal Tuesday morning.

Once our visitors had all gone, I tried to settle the children. It was a useless effort, work did not enter their minds, how could it when they were full of policemen? Remembering the phrase, 'If you can't beat 'em join 'em', I gathered my charges together to discuss policemen. It was a lively half hour. Each child seemed to have plenty to say on the subject, I suggested they sat down to write about it. This is what they had to say:

Nicola Smith: 'Policemen take people in to cort and asck peoplel questions and sometimes they put them in jail and check their pockets.'

David McCullough: 'Policemen are very good because they can send out a surch party when you are lost, and they chase cars.'

Carl Morgan: 'Police have this gun it tells you how fast the cars go. The policemen have walkie talkies for emergencies.'

Paul Rosser: 'The police have to catch criminals like the Yorkshire Ripper.'

Mark Elliot: 'Police are good because if people are bad the police arrest them and put them in jail. They take fingerprints.'

Douglas Cain: 'If your Mam and Dad bash you the police come and take them away.'

I thought PC Jackson might like to hear these opinions of his work. I asked him if he could come to a school assembly, hoping he would talk about his job. Bravely he accepted my invitation.

On the day of this special assembly, there was an air of great excitement. The children had practised saying their pieces loud enough for a policeman to hear. We were well prepared. One child, Bethan Walton, wrote a prayer for policemen. It went, 'Dear God. Please look after the policemen. Give them your blessing and protection. Amen.'

We waited and waited. No policeman appeared. The headmistress decided to begin without him. Everyone was certain he would eventually arrive. The children read their passages with one eye on the door, expecting at any moment, to see Peter Jackson. PC Jackson did not come. Imaginations began to run riot.

'He's had an accident.'

'He's chasing robbers.'

'There's been a murder.'

'Praps he's been shot.'

Only the most urgent of business could keep PC Jackson away from our assembly.

Two days later, PC Jackson came, alive and well to give his talk. He apologised for letting us down. His car had given him trouble. This simple explanation did not make him less interesting in the eyes of the children. They sat shiny-eyed, waiting to hear what he had to say. There can be no doubt that his visit was a great success. The proof being in the accounts written by them.

Thomas Hardy: 'Yesterday Peter came to our hall and he showed us his radio and his handcuffs and showed us his whistle. They were good and he put his helmet on us and I asked him if he had been hit on the head but he said they did not get chance to hit him and then me and Graham took him to the door and he did a skid for us in his car.'

Kevin McDonald: 'Yesterday Peter came to our school he came in his uniform. He came in a green car he had a whistle and handcuffs and a walky talky. He had a big helmet Tom could try it on so could I. We even measured him he was 1 metre 80 centimetres. He put his handcuffs on Tom and Jonathan and Lee. I asked him a question I asked him what is the biggest force in the world. He said American. He had to think before he answered me.'

Carol Berry: 'PC Jackson's helmet was too big for Stephen and it was just right for Tom and Mrs. Duffy said to him walk up to the top of the hall and back so Tom walked to the top of the hall with the helmet on his head.'

Sharon White: 'PC Jackson let Kieran have a go of his whistle and Jonathan have a go of his handcuffs.'

Iain Johnstone: 'Jonathan had a go of the handcuffs he slipped out of the handcuffs we all laughed.'

David McCullough: 'He told us about road safety and he told us what he did in the police station.'

Stephen Pettit: 'PC Jackson came to our school. He is the policeman for Harrington and the Queen.'

Shortly after Peter's visit, I was told that 'our cop' had been chasing a man outside school. I thought someone's imagination was overactive. When 30 other children confirmed this information, I thought perhaps there may be some truth in it. What a cynical woman I must be. PC Jackson was chasing a badie—a thief no less. From that day Peter the policeman became fixed as a hero in the minds of 105 mixed infants.

Walking Harrington beat will never be the same. No peace for contemplative strolls with dozens of children daring to talk to 'our cop'. Thanks to him we haven't missed our stolen television.

*     *     *

The following is a letter sent by a firm of Solicitors to the County Prosecuting Solicitor:

We are only very recently in receipt of the Depositions with a view to our client's committal to the Crown Court and the same are currently under review. Prior to the forthcoming hearing of Thursday of this week the 25th February, we anticipate being in a position to indicate our agreement or otherwise to the short form of commital procedure.

However, as a result of our consideration of the papers thus far, we have to tell you that we take strong exception to the words "the offender" as contained in the first page of the statement of Detective Constable Jones and in the first page of the statement of Detective Constable Smith (pages 6 and 12 of the Depositions respectively). To put it mildly, such a gratuituously pejorative description of the defendant can be said to betray an over-weaning confidence on the part of the Prosecution. It is clearly prejudicial and inadmissable. Fortunately, this gratuitous insult can be easily expunged by the deletion of these two words from each of the offending statements and we take it that the prosecution will readily confirm its agreement to this course being adopted. We await hearing from you.

Yours faithfully

A copy of this letter was sent to the chief constable by the County Prosecuting Solicitor together with the accompanying letter:

**Prosecutions Police—Use of the word 'offender'**

I send herewith a copy of the letter I have recently received. Whilst I cannot get as excited about the use of the word 'offender' in this context as my correspondent I must agree that its use is not proper. Please advise your officers to use the word 'defendant' — if only out of respect for the blood pressure of equally sensitive defenders.

Yours faithfully

*        *        *

**Extract from the Derby Evening Telegraph**
## COMMENT

The Commissioner of the Metropolitan Police, Sir David McNee is to retire. There is considerable speculation concerning the identity of his successor. The choice will be of particular interest in view of the current debate concerning the accountability of chiefs of police.

An advertisement to attract the right sort of successor for Sir David will have to be carefully framed. If the job of drafting is left to some of the most vociferous critics of the police, it might read something like this:

'Experienced police person required as figurehead for the Metropolitan police force. The successful applicant will have a degree in sociology and a doctorate of Political Awareness. He will have a working knowledge of the 24 foreign languages, 32 dialects and 14 sub-dialects of the ethnic minorities within the Greater London area and liaise closely with the 152 spokespeople for these groups.

'He will maintain close links with non-radically based minority groups and have regular meaningful discourse with the elected representatives of the people of London (i.e. local councillors).

'He will ensure that the principles of democracy are maintained by preventing extremist groups (i.e. Social Democratic Party, the Conservative Party, the National Association for Freedom and the Campaigners for Heterosexual Rights) from provoking and exploiting the masses.

'Remuneration is considerable. An attractive uniform (dark

blue overalls, matching shirt and tie, black beret and kid gloves) is provided free. Other fringe benefits include: Chauffeur driven BSA motor-bike, weekly directives from committee chairpersons of the Greater London Council, free subscriptions to Labour Weekly, the National Council for Civil Liberties, Gay News and the Ken Livingstone Appreciation Society.

'It is a condition of employment that the appointee consent to minor brain surgery to facilitate the implanting of a Kowtow microprocessor, which will be linked to the central computer of the GLC political secretariat.

'FOOTNOTE: A proven ability to catch criminals and prevent crime may be an advantage.'

★        ★        ★